Understanding Oregon's Gun Laws

A Guide To Gun Ownership In Plain English

Kevin Starrett

With Material By Culture Wars Associates

Creative Crisis Management Publishing
Box 556
Canby, Oregon 97013

Creative Crisis Publishing
PO Box 556
Canby OR 97013
(503) 263-5830

Cover photo: Kevin Starrett
Design: Anita Jones, Another Jones Graphics

ISBN 13: 978-0-9774939-3-7

Attention: Instructors, clubs, organizations, and interested parties,
please contact us for quantity discounts.

Printed and bound in the United States.

This book is dedicated to the amazing members of the Oregon Firearms Federation, whose tireless activism has preserved gun rights in Oregon.

Acknowledgments

The late Paul Deparrie, author, activist, crusader, contributed much of the chapter on dealing with a handgun license revocation, which originally appeared on the web page of the Oregon Firearms Federation.

The Oregon Firearms Federation and all the many people who support it created an environment where there are still some freedoms to write about. Nothing would be possible without their commitment to gun rights. I wish I could thank each one personally.

Table of Contents

"The great object is that every man be armed.. Every one who is able may have a gun."

—Patrick Henry

Introduction

"The right of the people to keep and bear arms shall not be infringed."

What could be more clear? If only it were so.

A hundred or more years of crooked politicians, politically moti-vated judges and self-serving "special interest" groups have eroded this fundamental right to a point where none of our founders would recognize it.

If they were here to witness how far we have slid down the road to serfdom, they would be heartbroken.

Your "right" to be armed has degenerated into a "privilege" that is regulated, restricted, licensed, limited, taxed and often just elimi-nated.

It is the opinion of this author that any law that reduces the rights of Americans to own and carry the firearm of their choice is unconstitutional and illegitimate.

But the fact remains that thousands of laws of this kind are on the books in our country, and too many judges have shown predictably little interest in reading the plain language of our Bill of Rights.

In fact, if our experience in court is any indication, they have shown very little interest in reading the laws that pertain to any case with which they are dealing.

With that in mind, it's the purpose of this book to examine and explain the gun laws of Oregon, while making no attempt to support their legitimacy.

Although Oregon has gun laws that are not as bad as some states', the fact is that many people, including politicians and law enforce-ment officers, simply don't understand them.

Since 1991, first as a representative of Gun Owners of America, and then as the director of the Oregon Firearms Federation, I have had the opportunity to deal with Oregon gun laws in many ways.

I have testified at countless legislative hearings concerning gun laws. I have been a guest on scores of radio and TV shows and I have

1

had the opportunity to help instruct many people, not only in the safe handling of their firearms, but also in a better understanding of what the law actually says. The amount of misinformation out there is staggering.

Unfortunately, much of it is coming from "experts" who are teaching other gun owners. A lot of what they are teaching is just plain wrong.

This book will explain, in simple, layman's terms, what the law actually says. It will also describe some of the many ways the law has been twisted by tax-funded bureaucrats.

Knowledge is power. Knowing the facts is essential in a world where many people, including people in positions of power and authority, do not look kindly on people who carry guns for the defense of themselves and others.

Obviously this book is not legal advice. I am not a lawyer, although the organizations I work for have spent a ton of money on them. But here's some advice I am happy to give.

If you carry a gun, or plan to, know the law, and know a lawyer. I have seen too many heartbreaking examples of honest, well-meaning people who have been railroaded by a system that chews up and spits out those who lack knowledge and resources. I recommend in addition to knowing a local attorney who is knowledgeable about gun laws, that you consider one of the pre-paid legal plans. They may not provide a brilliant lawyer, but they are available 24 hours a day nationwide. If you suddenly find yourself needing legal help, it's not likely to be at a time or place where your lawyer is available.

If you find yourself at odds with the system, the more you know, the better your chances of emerging from the other end of the ordeal reasonably intact. But it still won't be pleasant.

Having the name and phone number of a competent attorney who believes in your rights, and having the presence of mind to understand when that lawyer should be speaking for you, is every bit as important as your choice of revolver versus semi-auto, or .9mm versus .45.

But even if you never find yourself in trouble, knowing the facts about the law makes you a better, more responsible gun owner. It allows you to set the record straight when faced with the false information that's out there, and it helps you be a respected voice for gun rights.

The sad truth is, you cannot count on your local police to tell you what the law is. All too often, they don't know. The Oregon Firearms

Federation interviewed every sheriff's office in the state and found their knowledge of the law was often abysmal.

In hearings in the Oregon Legislature, representatives of law enforcement have testified that they got no training on the concealed handgun license law. In some cases, they willingly distort the truth. In some cases they just don't know it.

This book will explain what the law actually says. It will give you the exact wording of the law along with a plain language summary.

Of course, laws change. While every effort has been made to keep this book as up-to-date as possible, you should be aware of changes in the law that may affect your rights. Keep in mind that laws change not only through acts of the legislature, but by rulings of courts. These are often the hardest to track.

It has been my great fortune to have worked for an organization that fights tirelessly for the rights of gun owners. But the real work has been done by gun owners across the state and the country who did all the heavy lifting by making politicians hear their voices.

To all the people who supported our efforts with their contributions and their willingness to scream bloody murder when their rights were being attacked, I am truly grateful. You are my brothers and sisters in this battle, and I know we would have accomplished nothing without you. Be proud. You've done much.

Read this book through and keep it handy. When you're done you'll be more knowledgeable about Oregon gun laws than most lawmakers.

"The right of self defence is the first law of nature: in most governments it has been the study of rulers to confine this right within the narrowest limits possible. Wherever ...the right of the people to keep and bear arms is under any color or pretext whatsoever, prohibited, liberty, if not already annihilated, is on the brink of destruction."

—St. George Tucker
Federal Judge under President James Madison

Chapter 1

The Rules

An Overview

Most of the rules about gun ownership in Oregon are in the Oregon Revised Statutes, also known as the "ORS." The "statutes" are the rules made by the legislature. In theory, they are the supreme law of the state.

The statutes dealing with guns and gun ownership are in Section 166, starting at 166.170 and ending at 166.663. (There are a few other places where guns are mentioned. For example, the traffic code forbids riding an ATV or a snowmobile with a loaded gun, and there is a trespass statute that includes guns.)

The statutes are available online at:
http://www.leg.state.or.us/ors/166.html

They are also available at any law library, which can be found at many colleges and courthouses. A complete copy appears at the back of this book.

There are other places where rules dealing with guns exist however. The Oregon Administrative Rules and the ordinances of localities like counties and cities also deal with gun possession and use.

The Administrative Rules are available online at:
http://arcweb.sos.state.or.us/banners/rules.htm

"Administrative Rules" are rules made up by bureaucrats with the permission of the legislature.

For example, the legislature might give the authority to the Forest Service to make rules about the State Forests. Often, the legislature makes the broader laws and leaves it up to agencies to work out the details.

As you might expect, given an opportunity to make rules, bureaucrats almost always go hog wild making as many rules as they can, even when they make no sense and conflict with the law.

This sad fact of life is the cause for much of the confusion in Oregon law, as legislators write rules dealing with firearms and the unelected bureaucrats immediately come up with their *own* rules that say the exact opposite of what the legislature had in mind.

In most cases, the legislators never bother to read the Administrative Rules and are completely unaware that these contradictory rules exist. It often seems like the bureaucrats never read the laws before they write the rules.

It's not until some innocent gun owner finds himself in trouble for obeying the law that any of this comes to light, and then, court cases and huge legal bills usually ensue. I know of gun owners who were arrested for actions that were entirely lawful.

The third and most complicated depository of gun rules lies in the murky world of local ordinances.

Although Oregon has a "preemption" law that says that only the State Legislature can make rules about firearms possession, there are exceptions. Those exceptions rear their ugly little heads early in the gun statutes at 166.170, the part of the law that defines "preemption." They create a loophole large enough to drive a Howitzer through.

You can read that section in its entirety at the back of the book.

What the section means is that counties and cities *may* regulate the public possession of loaded guns with a few exceptions.

The problem, of course, is determining just what the rules are in the place you happen to be.

In most of the state, for example, carrying a loaded handgun without a permit is legal as long as it's not concealed. But should you stray into, let's say, the City of Beaverton, you would be violating Beaverton Ordinance 5.08.24 which makes it a class A misdemeanor to have a loaded gun in a public place if you don't have a concealed handgun license.

The 2010 "Oregon Blue Book" lists over 250 "incorporated cities" and Oregon has 36 counties. As you can imagine, it's impossible to know what the rules in each of these localities are. As you might expect, there is no central clearing house for this information. Furthermore, localities don't post gun rules like they post traffic rules.

So, with that in mind, I will now walk you through the laws that are actually in statute and, wherever possible, warn you about the hard-to-find rules that may, or may not, apply to you.

Chapter 2

Possessing Guns In Oregon

The rules dealing with who may possess a firearm are in section 166.250. It should be noted that there are no permits to possess or purchase firearms in Oregon. Furthermore, there is no system of registration of firearms in Oregon, except the *de facto* registration that accompanies a purchase from a Federally licensed dealer. (FFL)

Here's the short version of who may possess guns, followed by some explanations.

Keep in mind, there are exceptions to almost everything.

First: You must be 18. (Usually)

Second: You may not have a felony record or have been convicted of certain crimes while you were a minor. (More on this later.)

Third: You must have no convictions for misdemeanor "domestic violence."

Fourth: You must not have a history of mental illness.

That being said, under certain circumstances, a minor (someone under the age of 18) may possess a firearm, other than a handgun, if he got it with his parent's permission and he is not prohibited for other reasons.

Furthermore, a minor may use a firearm (including a handgun) "temporarily, for hunting or target shooting, or any lawful purpose." The law separates those two classes. So, if a minor borrowed a gun for "hunting or target shooting, or any lawful purpose" the requirement that they have their parent's permission would not apply.

According to Oregon law, anyone 18 or over who is not prohibited for any of the reasons listed above, may have a handgun in his home or "place of business." For the purposes of this law, "home" includes a recreational vessel or recreational vehicle. This is true for both residents of Oregon and those "temporarily sojourning within this state."

Be aware, the Oregon Supreme Court has found that "place of business" does not mean "where you work." The court's position is that in order for a location to be "your place of business," you must own the business. An interesting interpretation and not by any means the strangest the Oregon Courts have come up with. (See State of Oregon vs Perry.)

It's important to note that these are the laws that restrict gun possession in the eyes of Oregon law. There are other rules that prohibit people from possessing guns based on Federal law. For example, persons with misdemeanor convictions for "domestic violence" and persons who use illegal drugs, or persons who have had dishonorable discharges from the military. (See Title 18 USC § 922 (g))

Federal law prohibits anyone under 21 from purchasing a handgun or a "pistol grip" shotgun from a licensed firearms dealer, and possession of a handgun by persons under 18 requires written approval of a parent or guardian. (18 USC§922 (x))

Unlawful possession of a firearm is a Class A misdemeanor.

As stated above, persons with felony convictions are generally prohibited from owning guns. There are exceptions however. Those are listed in ORS 166.270 and 166.274

The felon in possession law does not apply to a person who was:

(a) Convicted of only one felony under the law of this state or any other state, or who has been convicted of only one felony under the laws of the United States, which felony did not involve criminal homicide, as defined in ORS 163.005, or the possession or use of a firearm or a weapon having a blade that projects or swings into position by force of a spring or by centrifugal force, and who has been discharged from imprisonment, parole or probation for said offense for a period of 15 years prior to the date of alleged violation of subsection (1) of this section; or

(b) Granted relief from the disability under 18 U.S.C. 925(c) or ORS 166.274 or has had the person's record expunged under the laws of this state or equivalent laws of another jurisdiction.

This is an interesting section of the law and the cause of an amazing amount of confusion. Here is the problem. While it is true that this section means that a person described above cannot be charged with "felon in possession" they still may not own firearms. While the "felon in possession" statute no longer applies, they are still prohibited from owning firearms under 166.250, which is the misdemeanor unlawful possession statute. The amount of misunderstanding this rule has created is staggering. I have spoken to countless lawyers, legislators and even District Attorneys who have gotten this wrong. I got it wrong in previous editions of this book. 15 years after parole or probation, a person with a felony record does not automatically get his gun rights restored.

Federal law prohibits possession of firearms or ammunition by persons who have been convicted of any crime "punishable" by a term of more than one year. (Title 18 §922 [g]) Furthermore, it is also illegal to transfer a firearm to a person who is under indictment for any crime punishable by more than one year. (Title 18 § 922 [d])

Oregon law does allow certain felons to petition to get their gun rights back. This is an area of law that caused a giant battle in the Oregon Legislature in a "special" session in 2010. (Be warned, it is very likely this part of the law may be changed again soon. Please check the most recent ORS.)

In 2009, we requested a bill that would correct an anomaly in Oregon law. Prior to the enactment of SB 603 in 2009, Oregon law allowed persons with felony convictions to petition the court to have their rights restored to buy a gun. The problem was, (again few people understood this) while the law allowed you to request the right to buy a gun, you still could not *own* a gun!

After months of explanations and wrangling, we convinced the Chair of the Senate Judiciary Committee that this could not possibly be what the legislature had in mind. He finally agreed and that error was corrected in SB 603 which took effect in January of 2010. That bill passed both the House and Senate without a single "no" vote and was signed by the Governor. The Senate actually passed it twice. An awful lot of lawyers looked at the bill during the process and not a single person had a single objection. The most militant gun haters in the legislature voted "yes." Then in September of 2009, after the bill had passed, but before it went into effect in January of 2010, the Department of Justice had a meltdown and came to the legislature asking that it be overturned, because it was a "mistake" that would allow felons to "walk out of prison and be handed guns."

That accusation was absurd of course. The bill did nothing of the kind. But in the 2010 "special session" a chaotic and baffling battle took place to reverse that element of SB 603. The very person who drafted the bill, Senator Floyd Prozanski, was now working overtime to reverse it. The battle, while in some ways comical, demonstrated the vast and disturbing ignorance of the legislative body, all of whom misunderstood both SB 603 and the bills introduced to overturn it.

After a bruising battle, the new bill (SB 1064) was amended in the House and kept SB 603 intact except for one minor change.

ORS 167.274 describes how a person with a felony conviction can petition for rights restoration. You can read the actual language in the back of this book, although for a number of reasons you may find it very confusing.   Basically the law requires that you go to a Circuit Court and make a case for yourself. The one change from SB 603 that took place in the 2010 special session was this: SB 603 allowed the petitioner to go to "Justice Court." Now he must file in Circuit Court. See page 138 for a sample petition for rights restoration.

Section 7 of 166.274 deals specifically with persons who were minors when their offense was committed.

"A person barred from possessing or purchasing a firearm because the person, while a minor, was found to be within the jurisdiction of the juvenile court for committing an act which, if committed by an adult, would have constituted a felony or a misdemeanor involving violence, is not eligible to petition for relief under this section until more than four years have passed since the person was discharged from the jurisdiction of the juvenile court."

This means that if you committed your crime as a juvenile, you must wait 4 years to petition for rights restoration.

Be aware however, that there are tremendous Federal roadblocks to rights restoration if you were convicted of a Federal offense.

What follows is an exact copy of the question about rights restoration and the answer from the website of the Federal Bureau of Alcohol, Tobacco, Firearms and Explosives:

(A10)

Q. *How can a person convicted of a felony apply for relief from firearms disabilities?*

A. *Under the provisions of the Gun Control Act of 1968 (GCA), convicted felons and certain other persons are prohibited from possessing firearms. (See 18 U.S.C. section 922(g).) The GCA provides the Secretary of the Treasury with the authority to grant relief from this disability where the Secretary determines that the person is not likely to act in a manner dangerous to the public safety. (See 18 U.S.C. section 925(c).) The Secretary delegated this authority to ATF.*

Since October 1992, however, ATF's annual appropriation has continuously prohibited the expending of any funds to investigate or act upon applications for relief from Federal firearms disabilities. This restriction is located in Pub. L. No. 107-67, 115 Stat. 514, which contains ATF appropriations for fiscal year 2002. As long as this provision is included in current ATF appropriations, the Bureau cannot act upon applications for relief from Federal firearms disabilities submitted by individuals. Consequently, we cannot entertain any individual's request for firearms restoration while this prohibition on the processing of such applications remains in place.

Furthermore, the restriction contained in Pub. L. No. 107-67 does not change the status of prohibited persons. They are still prohibited from possessing, receiving, transporting, or shipping firearms under Federal law.

(A11)

Q. *Are there any alternatives for relief from firearms disabilities?*

A. *Current alternatives as follows:*

Persons convicted of a Federal offense may apply for a Presidential pardon. Sections 1.1 through 1.10 of the Code of Federal Regulations, Title 28, specify the rules governing petitions for obtaining Presidential pardons. You may contact the Pardon Attorney's Office at the U.S. Department of Justice, 500 First Street, NW., Washington, DC 20530, to inquire about the procedures for obtaining a Presidential pardon.

Persons convicted of a State offense may contact the State Attorney General's Office within the State in which they reside for information concerning any alternatives that may be available.

The short version of this is that because anti-gun politicians continually refuse to allow the BATFE to have the funds to determine if a person's rights should be restored, it isn't happening, and won't until the law is changed. But, although there is quite a bit of dispute and disagreement about this, many lawyers believe that if your rights are restored by the state, as they can be under current Oregon law, the Feds will recognize this and allow you to own firearms.

"Domestic Violence"

In 1996, one of the most abusive and abused laws ever written to attack gun ownership was passed.

Commonly known as the "Lautenberg Amendment," the law prohibits *anyone* who has ever been convicted of a misdemeanor crime of "domestic violence" from ever owning a firearm or a single round of ammunition for the rest of his or her life.

The law was retroactive, which meant that if you pled guilty to a misdemeanor crime of "domestic violence" 40 years ago, you still lost your rights.

Many people are unaware of this or unaware that if they own a firearm and had a past conviction, they are felons.

In many cases, people who were involved in minor incidents that, in the past, would have been resolved without police intervention have been arrested and charged with crimes of "domestic violence."

Often, they were told by prosecuting attorneys that the problem would "go away" if they pled to a "minor" charge of misdemeanor domestic violence and paid a small fine or agreed to a short stint of community service or "anger management" classes.

Many did so in order to put the matter behind them and avoid ruinous attorney's fees.

What they were **not** told was what they would lose for their willingness to comply with the heavy-handed tactics of DAs. They would lose their gun rights...forever.

In 2007, Oregon passed Senate Bill 81. This bill required that before a person can plead guilty to a charge of "domestic violence" he must be informed that he will lose his gun rights forever. A step in the right direction to be sure, but little solace to all those who lost their rights before the bill was signed because of the unscrupulous behavior of some "officers of the court." Persons who have lost their rights under this law have a few options including requesting an expungement or seeking rights restoration under 166.274.

Types Of Firearms Allowed

Oregon has no restriction on any conventional firearm. This means there are no restrictions on any firearm not covered under the National Firearms Act, which is discussed below. Oregon has no restrictions on so called "assault weapons" or large capacity magazines. If it's not covered by the NFA, you are free to buy and own it without restriction.

NFA Firearms

NFA firearms and other items restricted by Federal law such as suppressors (silencers) are legal to own in Oregon.

These include machine guns, the frames and receivers of machine guns or parts designed or intended to be used for converting weapons to full auto, short-barreled rifles, shotguns and silencers. However, these devices usually require the permission of the chief law enforcement agent in your area, typically the county sheriff. You will be required to comply with all Federal laws to have legal possession. You can download the BATFE regulations for all the rules for owning guns that turn money into noise at this website:
http://www.access.gpo.gov/nara/cfr/waisidx_09/27cfr479_09.html

ORS 166.210 defines "short-barreled rifles and shotguns." Guns meeting these specifications require Federal approval. They also require permission from your chief local law enforcement agent, typically your county sheriff. There are ways around this however. NFA firearms may also be purchased by corporations and "trusts" and those purchases can be made without the sheriff's approval. You still need Federal approval however. You can download a guide to NFA firearms created by the ATF here:
http://www.atf.gov/publications/download/p/atf-p-5320-8/atf-p-5320-8.pdf

(8) "Short-barreled rifle" means a rifle having one or more barrels less than 16 inches in length and any weapon made from a rifle if the weapon has an overall length of less than 26 inches.

(9) "Short-barreled shotgun" means a shotgun having one or more barrels less than 18 inches in length and any weapon made from a shotgun if the weapon has an overall length of less than 26 inches. [Amended by 1977 c.769 §1; 1979 c.779 §3; 1989 c.839 §1; 1993 c.735 §14; 1995 c.670 §3; 1999 c.1040 §2; 2001 c.666 §§32,44; 2003 c.614 §7]

Here is an interesting factoid. While Oregon law defines "short barreled rifle" and "short barreled shotgun," it does NOT define "rifle" and "shotgun." According to Federal law, a shotgun is: *a weapon designed or redesigned, made or remade, and intended to be fired from the shoulder and designed or redesigned and made or remade to use the energy of an explosive to fire through a smooth bore either a number of ball shot or a single projectile for each single pull of the trigger."*

So then, what is a pistol-grip shotgun? According to ATF it's not a "shotgun" at all. It's hard to get them to tell you what it is, but at least one ATF publication says it is a "pistol-grip firearm." These may not be sold to anyone under 21. But many dealers don't know this. To further confuse things, if you shorten the barrel on a "shotgun" to under 18 inches, you are now in possession of a "short-barreled shotgun" which requires a $200.00 tax stamp to be legal. But if you shorten the barrel of a shotgun that came from the factory with a pistol grip, you are now in possession of "any other weapon" which requires a $5.00 tax stamp to be legal. But what if you put a rifled barrel on a shotgun? Is it still a shotgun? Federal law would seem to indicate that it's now a rifle. What do you have if you shorten a rifled barrel on a pistol grip shotgun? At the time this book went to print, we were still awaiting answers from the ATF to those questions.

"To preserve liberty, it is essential that the whole body of the people always possess arms, and be taught alike, especially when young, how to use them."

—Richard Henry Lee
Signer of the Declaration of Independence

Chapter 3

Purchasing Guns In Oregon

In Oregon firearms may be purchased from licensed dealers or from private parties.

Dealer Transfers

The rules dealing with a purchase from a Federal Firearms License holder are explained in ORS 166.412. Persons forbidden from buying firearms are described in ORS 166.470.

In order to purchase a firearm from a gun dealer, you must provide the dealer with identification. That identification must be issued by a government entity and include a photo and your birth date.

You must be a resident of Oregon to buy a handgun. If you are not an Oregon resident, you may only purchase a handgun if the gun is shipped to a licensed dealer in the state in which you reside. (Note, Federal law also allows you to purchase if you are a "corporation or other business entity" and you maintain "a place of business" in the state. But demonstrating that to the satisfaction of most dealers might be a problem.)

You may purchase a long gun if you live in another state and your purchase does not violate that state's rules. See USC Title 18 922 (b) [3]

There is considerable confusion about buying a firearm, particularly a handgun, if you own homes in more than one state and your driver's license is from a state other than Oregon.

The Federal Regulations Reference Book, published by the Bureau of Alcohol, Tobacco, Firearms and Explosives specifically addresses this in the "Questions and Answers" section. They quite clearly state that it is legal to purchase a handgun in the state in which you are "residing" even if you have a driver's license from another state. The State Police have told us that they will approve a firearms purchase for a person with a driver's license from another state, if that person has some documentation that they reside in Oregon, such as a lease. If you find yourself in that situation, it will serve you well to have a copy of the above mentioned regulations book (available on the BATFE's website) and a copy of the Oregon law. Contrary to what has been written elsewhere, there is no minimum amount of time you must be a resident of Oregon before you may purchase a gun. If you can demonstrate that you live in Oregon, you may purchase at any time.

You must submit to a background check, for which you pay $10.00 and you must provide thumbprints. (This fee may go up, so check the latest rules.)

In many states, the dealer contacts the "National Instant Check System," operated by the FBI. There is no charge and information about the gun is not collected. In Oregon however, you must contact the State Police, and pay the fee.

Furthermore the dealer must provide the State Police with the make, model, caliber and serial number of the gun you buy. The law allows the police to keep this information for a maximum of 5 years, however, there is no penalty if they keep this information any longer. The gun dealer must keep your thumbprints for 5 years as well.

The background check performed by the State Police is, in theory, "instant."In many cases, it actually is relatively fast. The approval comes either immediately, while the dealer is on his initial call to the State Police for approval, or shortly afterward in a return call.However, there are many cases where the background check is anything but "instant."

The law requires that the State Police provide a "unique authorization number" for an approval of sale, or notify the dealer that the sale is prohibited, within 30 minutes. If they are unable to provide that information within 30 minutes, they must provide an estimate of how long it will take to provide it. The law does not place a limit on how long that may be. However, the law also states that if no authorization number or notice of disqualification is given by "close of business, the day after the request for a background check was made," the dealer _may_ transfer the firearm. Keep in mind, Federal law overrides state law for transfers without authorization numbers. Federal law requires three business days to "transpire" before a transfer may take place without an authorization. According to the BATF a business day is *"any 24-hour day beginning at 12:01 a.m. the day after the check was initiated, on which state offices are open. A business day does not include Saturday, Sunday, or holidays."* So if your background check was done on a Monday, and there was no "approval," Tuesday, Wednesday and Thursday must "transpire" and you may lawfully take possession on Friday.

In conversations we have had with the State Police ID Unit, they have informed us that dealers almost never transfer under those circumstances. That opinion has been reinforced by dealers we have spoken with. This may be due to an ignorance of the law, or a fear of the possible repercussions.

In the past, delays and denials often happened to people who were qualified for purchase. At one time the State Police ID unit often told buyers and dealers that they could not transfer without an approval code. In fact, the State Police provided gun dealers with a handbook that contained this error. After several meetings between OFF and the State Police, this situation seems to have improved dramatically.

The State Police told this author that the backlog of delays is due to demands by the FBI that they do more intrusive background checks looking for persons with "domestic violence" convictions. (As stated earlier, a misdemeanor domestic violence conviction prohibits a person from owning a firearm or a single round of ammunition for life.)

Countless persons with no criminal record of any kind have been the victims of this failed system. With the expansion of the Brady Law through an NRA supported bill, HR 2640, signed by President Bush in January of 2008, it's safe to assume the problem will get worse. In June of 2009, the Oregon Legislature passed HB 2853. This bill created a system to force Oregon into compliance with the federal bill. Its actual implementation will depend on available funding. If implemented, it will require those who been erroneously flagged as "mental defectives" to seek relief from the "Psychiatric Review Board."

An item of interest here is that if you check ORS 166.412, you will see that the background provisions once related only to handgun transfers. However, if you continue to ORS 166.434, you'll see that the rules were extended to all guns.

Private transfers

Private transfers of firearms, within the state of Oregon, are largely unregulated except at "gun shows."

If you (as a private party) sell or otherwise transfer a conventional firearm to another non-prohibited person, there is no required notification of the police, no registration, no permit to purchase or possess and no mandatory background check.

The law is different at gun shows.

At this point, (thanks to a ballot measure passed by Oregon voters who had been hoodwinked by a multimillion dollar, anti-gun ad campaign starring John McCain) things get very confusing. First, a little history.

The absolutely hare-brained law dealing with private transfers at gun shows was the result of a failed attempt to attack gun owners rights in the 1999 legislative session.

That year, Democratic Senator Ginny Burdick attempted to ban private sales at gun shows.

Burdick had long been known for having a single-minded obsession with gun control. She had the support of the Republican leadership of the Republican controlled Senate that helped her pass her bill.

When her bill moved over to the House, (which was also controlled by Republicans) Democrat-turned-Republican Representative Kevin Mannix announced his desire to draft a bill that would "satisfy" both gun owners and gun haters.

At Oregon Firearms Federation, we were, to say the least, skeptical.

So, after some wrangling and the predictable hand wringing by the gun control fanatics, Mannix got Burdick's bill tabled and wrote his own version. In closed-door meetings with representatives of the establishment gun lobby, (including both a major national group and a local group) Mannix wrote a new bill.

(Representatives of Oregon Firearms Federation were barred from the meetings.)

After extensive negotiations with police groups, anti-gun organizations and the above mentioned "pro-gun" groups, Mannix managed to craft a bill that was even worse than the original bill sponsored by Burdick.

He also got both of the attending "gun groups" to go along with his bill. The national organization agreed not to object (and in fact did not even alert their members to the new bill) and the local organization embraced and promoted it. Oregon Firearms Federation continued to oppose it, and after passing in Oregon's House, the bill was killed by one vote when it went back to the Senate.

As a result of that loss, Burdick, fueled by millions of dollars from out-of-state anti-gun organizations, put the measure before voters as Ballot Measure 5 in 2000. The sloppily written measure was basically a rewrite of the sloppy bill that Mannix had written and is a testimony to the dangers of asking people to vote on issues that are never honestly explained.

Every major newspaper in Oregon blatantly misrepresented the content and intent of the ballot measure. Senator John McCain recorded TV commercials promoting it and the majority of voters in the Portland area, who wouldn't know a reasonable law if it threw itself off an overpass and landed on their Volkswagen bus, bought it. The measure failed in more counties than it passed, but it became law. It's interesting to note, that, in some ways, Burdick's ballot measure was not as bad as the bill Kevin Mannix and the "gun lobby" tried and failed to pass. The ballot measure changed the rules for private transfers, both at gun shows and elsewhere.

With that in mind, I will attempt to decipher what the law says, even when it's almost impossible to understand what it means. Let's discuss gun shows first.

If the transfer takes place at a "gun show" between two private parties, the background check is mandatory. The rules dealing with transfers by non-dealers appear in ORS 166.436 and 166.438.

Gun shows are described in Oregon law as being "an event at which more than 25 firearms are on site and available for transfer." Yes, this is a troublesome definition and one that is open to bizarre interpretations. (When the failed bill that led to this measure was being debated in the Legislature, the then head of the State Police ID unit was wandering the Capitol with a sticker on her blouse promoting the bill. You paid for her time there lobbying for more gun control. This may explain her refusal to respond to questions about their interpretation of the law. She has been, mercifully, replaced.)

Sales at gun shows by federally licensed dealers are the same as if the transfer was done at a store. Transfers between private parties at gun shows are explained below.

The State Police have produced a printed form (see Appendix, page 134) that gun show promoters must make available to any non-dealer selling a firearm at a gun show. The form is similar to the familiar 4473 form used by federally licensed gun dealers. When a sale of a firearm is made at a gun show, the buyer must complete the front page of the form giving the usual personal information and the seller must complete page two, which contains information about the gun, the type of ID used by the buyer and the response the State Police gave to the background check request.

The seller must call the State Police and request a background check on the buyer. The phone number for this check at the time this book was published was 800-432-5059. The seller will be required to provide his name and address. He must also provide the location where the transfer is taking place. The seller must also provide the name, date of birth, race and sex of the person to whom he is transferring the firearm.

He must provide information on the type of ID the buyer is using and the make, model, caliber and serial number of the firearm being transferred.

As with purchases from dealers, buyers may also voluntarily provide their social security number in the event that they don't feel that their privacy has been sufficiently invaded.

The cost for this "service" is $10.00 (at this time) and you must pay by credit card. If you do not have a credit card, you're out of luck. Attempts to dramatically raise this fee were killed by activist gun owners in the 2005 legislative session, but there have been continued efforts to increase the cost of the checks.

The State Police are then required to "immediately, or by return phone call" let the seller know if the buyer is qualified or prohibited from making the purchase. As with purchases from licensed dealers, the State Police have 30 minutes to provide the seller with a "yes" or "no" but if they cannot, the law requires them to give an estimate of how long it will take to provide that information.

If they give the go ahead, they will provide the seller with a unique authorization number. The approval number is described in the statute as "permit valid for 24 hours for the requested transfer." If the transfer is not made within 24 hours, the law requires that the seller must make a new request for a background check.

Of course, most gun shows run for just 2 or 3 days. In many cases the transfers can never take place because the State Police do not provide a response until the show is over and everyone has gone home.

Oregon law gives immunity from civil prosecution to sellers who have requested a background check, used the police-provided form and received authorization if the gun they sold is later used in a crime.

Note, nothing in Oregon law states that a transfer that was initiated at a gun show must take place there. So, for example, if a buyer and seller agreed to transfer a gun, and the transfer took place anywhere but the grounds of the gun show, such as the parking lot of a nearby burger joint, that transfer would be legal and require no background check, no paperwork, and no reporting.

Private transfers outside of gun shows do not require background checks. Individuals *may,* however, voluntarily run background checks on persons to whom they are transferring firearms. (The State Police have informed us that non-dealer background checks outside of gun shows virtually never happen.)

If you choose to conduct a background check and you are not at a gun show, (and as stated before, this almost never happens) you can use the same phone number to run the check as is used at gun shows, but you are not required to fill out the police-supplied form. Sellers outside of gun shows are provided with the same immunity from civil lawsuits, but get that immunity whether they have used the form or not. (It is rare for a person outside a gun show to have one of these forms, since they are usually only supplied by persons holding gun shows.)

The process is essentially the same. A call is made to the State Police, the information is given and the police are required to issue an authorization or denial within 30 minutes and if they do not, they must provide an estimate of how long it will take to do so. If an authorization is given, it's good for 24 hours.

The laws dealing with private transfers that involve the background check, either as required at gun shows, or as allowed away from gun shows differ from dealer transfers in an important way.

As stated earlier, if a licensed dealer does not get a response from the State Police, he may, after the specified time, proceed with the transfer anyway. There is no such provision for private transfers. Since gun shows usually only last 2 or 3 days, it does not come into play very much at those events. As for how it applies to private transfers where the background check is available but not mandatory, no one has any idea.

This is one area where the law really makes no sense. (As if any of this law made sense.) As noted above, according to section 166.436, if an individual who has requested this entirely "voluntary" background check fails to deliver the gun within 24 hours, he must make a new request for a background check.

However, no such background check is required to complete a non gun-show transfer in the first place. The steps mentioned above are strictly voluntary. So which is it? Is it voluntary to do a second background check or is it mandatory since you did the first background check? What happens if the background check is run, but the police don't respond? Can the transfer take place anyway just as it could if the transfer was being done by a dealer? The State Police have informed this author by e-mail that if a background check is done for a private transfer, and they do not respond in a timely fashion, the transfer may take place. Here is the exact quote from that e-mail:

> **In consultation with our Firearms Unit staff, if a private party (non-dealer or outside of a gun show) initiates a voluntary background check for a firearms transfer and receives a "pend", unless the seller has knowledge that the buyer is restricted (state or federal prohibition against purchasing or possessing a firearm), the seller can proceed to transfer the firearm without our approval.**
>
> **Let me know if you have any further questions.**
>
> **DCY**

Chapter 4

Carrying Guns in Oregon

The rules in Oregon that deal with carrying firearms are different for different people. (See ORS 166.250.) Let's divide them into several broad categories.

First you have people who may own guns and people who may not. In the previous chapters we discussed who may and may not own a gun. (This issue is complicated by the fact that it is possible to have an Oregon concealed handgun license but not be allowed to own a gun. For example, there have been several cases of persons who had medical marijuana licenses getting back their CHLs after court action, but those people are technically forbidden, by Federal law, from owning firearms. There are other examples of these kinds of contradictions.)

The next subdivision gives us "civilians" and everyone else. For the sake of discussing Oregon law, we can say that civilians are people who are not in law enforcement or the military. You can have a long and interesting debate about whether police and corrections officers are "civilians," but for the purposes of our discussion they must be treated as though they are not.

The exceptions for law enforcement and the military are spelled out in the statute. Police are exempt from most restrictions. Active duty military personal who are on duty are as well. So here, I will explain what is permitted and forbidden if you are not "on-duty" military or law enforcement.

Within the world of "civilians" we then have our final two categories: people with concealed handgun licenses and people without them. Oregon law treats them very differently.

I'll start with people who do not have licenses.

There is no *state* law that prohibits openly carrying a loaded firearm in most places. (I'll cover prohibited places later.) That means that in much of the state, the law does not forbid you from carrying both loaded handguns and loaded long guns.

For persons who do not have an Oregon concealed handgun license and are carrying, on their person, a firearm, loaded or not, the firearm may *not* be concealed. If you have a handgun in your car, loaded or not, and it is "readily accessible" it may *not* be concealed. You may however, have a loaded long gun in your car and it *may* be concealed.

To recap: On your body, if you have no license, you can't carry a concealed firearm loaded or unloaded.

That technically means that if you are coming home from a gun store with a new firearm, in a box, unloaded, you are breaking the law if you are "carrying" the gun. (Attempts to address this anomaly have been rejected numerous times by the Oregon State Legislature, but we know of no cases so far where a person has been charged under these circumstances.)

In your car, you may not have a "readily accessible" *concealed* handgun (loaded or unloaded) but you may have a concealed, loaded long gun.

Furthermore, ORS 821.240 forbids operating a snowmobile or ATV while in possession of a loaded firearm (or a bow, unless all the arrows are in the quiver.)

This applies whether the gun is concealed or not. (In several legislative sessions, efforts were made to define "loaded" as meaning a round was in the chamber. However, the anti-gun majority in the Senate refused to hear the bills.)

Breaking this rule is a Class B traffic violation. There is no exception to this rule for police. But, of course, they do it all the time. Please note that Oregon's definition of "ATV" goes well beyond quads and dirt bikes. ORS 801.193 defines a class II ATV as follows:

> **801.193 "Class II all-terrain vehicle."** *"Class II all-terrain vehicle"*
> *means any motor vehicle that:*
> *(1) Weighs more than a Class I all-terrain vehicle;*
> *(2) Is designed for or capable of cross-country travel on or immediately over land, water, sand, snow, ice, marsh, swampland or other natural terrain; and*
> *(3) Is actually being operated off a highway or is being operated on a highway for agricultural purposes under ORS 821.191. [1987 c.587 §2; 2005 c.227 §1; 2007 c.207 §1]*

This means that if you are off-roading in a Jeep or SUV, it is unlawful for your handgun to be loaded.

There is an interesting exception to the rule dealing with concealed handguns in vehicles however.

Although 166.250 (1) (b) says it's illegal to have a concealed handgun (without a handgun license) in any vehicle, it also says, in section (2) (B)[b], that this prohibition does not apply to *"a recreational vessel or recreational vehicle while used, for whatever period of time, as residential quarters."*

It is not clear by what is meant by "...whatever period of time, as residential quarters."

The law does not explain if you may have the gun concealed while you're stopped, but not while you're moving, or if you may conceal the handgun if you're driving, but someone else is napping or making lunch, hence using the vehicle as "residential quarters." Nor does it explain the meaning of "concealed." It's safe to assume that in a conventional car or truck, something is "not concealed" if a police officer can see it from outside. But how this applies to a motor home (where you might have a handgun easily visible to you on the bed or counter top, but not to a police officer who pulls you over) is not defined.

This being said, it is perfectly legal for a person who is not prohibited from owning a firearm, to carry a loaded handgun in his or her car, within reach, without a concealed handgun license, so long as the handgun is not concealed. *BUT,* Oregon law allows localities to restrict the carrying of loaded firearms for those who do not have a concealed handgun license. These restrictions may be applied in "public places." For many years most people, including this author, did not believe that they would apply to your car. Oregon law defines a "public place" as a place to which the "general public has access." Most of us believe that does not include our cars. But in December of 2008, the court found that your car is, for all intents and purposes a "public place" since in the court's opinion, your car is not a "place" at all, it is a "container" in a public place. So, in those places where loaded carry is restricted, those restrictions apply in your car as well for both long guns and handguns.

In some places, like Portland, not only must the firearm be unloaded, but all rounds must be removed from any magazine you are carrying as well.

In 2009, Oregon Firearms Federation passed SB 603 which finally defined what "readily accessible" means. The original language, as drafted by Oregon Firearm Federation, included a description of how a person could legally transport a handgun on a motorcycle. That language was removed from the final bill for no apparent reason. It may be added back in a future legislative session. As of 2010, the law defines "readily accessible" this way:

> **(4) (a) Except as provided in paragraph (b) of this subsection, a handgun is readily accessible within the meaning of this section if the handgun is within the passenger compartment of the vehicle.**
>
> **(b) If a vehicle has no storage location that is outside the passenger compartment of the vehicle, a handgun is not readily accessible within the meaning of this section if:**
>
> **(A) The handgun is stored in a closed and locked glove compartment, center console or other container; and**
>
> **(B) The key is not inserted into the lock, if the glove compartment, center console or other container unlocks with a key.**

You may wonder whether you can have a loaded firearm in a recreational vehicle (with no CHL) in those places like Portland and Salem that restrict loaded carry. Since state law specifically allows it, there is some question about whether local regulations can prohibit it. While I know of no case law that addresses this, it is the opinion of the lawyers at Legislative Counsel (the lawyers who write bills for the legislators) that local restrictions *would* apply. But what remains unresolved and (as far as I know) unlitigated, is whether there is a difference, legally speaking, between having a loaded handgun in an RV if you are using it as a vehicle or if you are using it as a residence.

There are several other exceptions to the law that prohibits non-licensees from carrying concealed firearms. (ORS 166.260) These are licensed hunters and fishermen, while hunting or fishing or traveling to, or returning from, hunting or fishing trips, and members of shooting clubs while at the clubs or traveling to and from those clubs.

A strong word of caution here. The courts have been very stingy with their interpretation of what "traveling to and from" means. In the case of State v. Thomas Foster, the court found that carrying a gun while en route to your beach house did not constitute traveling to or from a fishing trip, even if fishing was the purpose for going to the beach house.

If you are in possession of a concealed handgun and don't have a concealed handgun license, expect the courts to take a very narrow view of what traveling "to and from" means, should you interface with the law enforcement experience.

Prohibited And Non-Prohibited Places

There are places where unlicensed persons are forbidden from carrying guns, even if not concealed. These are covered under ORS 166.370 and deal with possession of guns in "public buildings."

Possession of a firearm in a public building without a concealed handgun license is a Class C felony.

ORS 166.360 defines "public buildings."

(4) "Public building" means a hospital, a capitol building, a public or private school, as defined in ORS 339.315, a college or university, a city hall or the residence of any state official elected by the state at large, and the grounds adjacent to each such building. The term also includes that portion of any other building occupied by an agency of the state or a municipal corporation, as defined in ORS 297.405, other than a court facility.

Federal law forbids people from having guns within 1000 feet of a school unless they are locked up or being used at a sanctioned event.

(Obviously, it is almost impossible to travel through any urban or suburban area without being within 1000 feet of a school, making this one of most ridiculous of Federal gun laws.) Oregon law has the same restrictions on school property.

In neither case do these prohibitions apply to license holders. Persons with concealed handgun licenses are *not* prohibited from being in public schools or on public school grounds with a concealed firearm.

Although many schools (and other public buildings) have posted signs warning that being on the posted property with a gun is prohibited, even for license holders, it is simply not true. If it were, anti-gun militants would not be returning to the Oregon legislature year after year demanding that new laws be passed to ban license holders from school property. (See Letter to Wayne Krieger, page 129.)

However, please note that both Federal law and Oregon law forbid discharging a firearm on school property except at sanctioned events. There is no exception for self defense unless you are a police officer.

The section of Federal law that exempts license holders from the Federal "Gun Free Schools" law is Title 18 § 922 (q).

ORS 166.370 also prohibits persons from having guns in "court facilities." Those are defined as follows:

(2) "Court facility" means a courthouse or that portion of any other building occupied by a circuit court, the Court of Appeals, the Supreme Court or the Oregon Tax Court or occupied by personnel related to the operations of those courts, or in which activities related to the operations of those courts take place.

Note, in both the case of "public buildings" and schools, license holders are exempt. However, license holders are *not* exempt from the prohibition in courthouses. Having a gun in a courthouse is a class C felony. You may notice that "Municipal Courts" are *not* included in the definition of "courts" listed above. Still, many Municipal Courts are posted with "No Firearms" signs. The Oregon Firearms Federation was a party to a lawsuit to block one city from posting such signs. The Circuit Court ruled that although the Municipal Court in question was not a "Court" for purposes of this statute, the signs could still be posted if that Court's judge wanted them there, because he can make whatever rules he wants for his courtroom. Presumably violating his rule would put you in contempt of court.

Airports around the state have signs warning that no weapons are allowed. The Portland Airport had such signs posted in the past. However, there is nothing in the law that allows a public airport to restrict firearms except beyond the security checkpoint. Oregon's Legislative Counsel, in a letter to House Majority Leader Wayne Scott, stated in no uncertain terms that the Port of Portland had no such authority. (See Letter to Wayne Scott, page 126.)

The Port of Portland used to enforce an ordinance they created that banned the carrying of firearms at the airport. After two sessions of having one of their pet bills defeated because of this ordinance, they rescinded it.

Federal law (Title 18 §930) also prohibits carrying firearms in "Federal facilities."

According to Federal law, the term "Federal facility" means: "a building or part thereof owned or leased by the Federal Government, where Federal employees are regularly present for the purpose of performing their official duties."

Much has been written about the apparent prohibition against carrying licensed concealed handguns in Post Offices. No doubt you have seen the ominous posters at most Post Offices warning against possessing firearms there. The posters cite Title 18 §930. However, they don't reproduce the entire section of that law. Here's what the poster includes:

(a) Except as provided in subsection (d), whoever knowingly possesses or causes to be present a firearm or other dangerous weapon in a Federal facility (other than a Federal court facility), or attempts to do so, shall be fined under this title or imprisoned not more than 1 year, or both.

(b) Whoever, with intent that a firearm or other dangerous weapon be used in the commission of a crime, knowingly possesses or causes to be present such firearm or dangerous weapon in a Federal facility, or attempts to do so, shall be fined under this title or imprisoned not more than 5 years, or both.

However, here is what the poster leaves out:

(d) Subsection (a) shall not apply to—
(1) the lawful performance of official duties by an officer, agent, or employee of the United States, a State, or a political subdivision thereof, who is authorized by law to engage in or supervise the prevention, detection, investigation, or prosecution of any violation of law;

(2) the possession of a firearm or other dangerous weapon by a Federal official or a member of the Armed Forces if such possession is authorized by law; or

(3) the lawful carrying of firearms or other dangerous weapons in a Federal facility incident to hunting or other lawful purposes.

Oregon law does not prohibit carrying guns in Post Offices. Licensed carry in Oregon is lawful. So, many have interpreted that licensed carry in an Oregon Post office is legal. Since previous editions of this book, I have become aware of one successful prosecution of a gun owner who possessed a firearm at a Post Office. In this case, Clarence Paul Dorosan was a Postal Service employee whose gun was in his car. He was convicted of breaking a "regulation" and not the "law." Dorosan appealed and on Oct 14th, 2009 lost. So it would be wise to consider Post Offices "off limits."

Private Property And The Workplace

Private property is private property, and if the owner of that property says that no guns are permitted, then they are not. Should you be on private property with a firearm and the owner asks you to leave, he is completely within his rights to do so. If you don't, you are trespassing. Furthermore, you are trespassing with a firearm, and as you will see, that is a crime in and of itself in Oregon. *(A court decision in Portland in 2007 ruled that your front porch is "public property" for purposes of charging someone with a gun possession violation. While we are confident that this bizarre and unsupportable decision will not stand up to further scrutiny, it demonstrates how fluid the concepts of "public" and "private"are.)*

Many people want to know if their employer can insist that they not have a firearm during work hours. The short answer is yes. There are several reasons for this. First, the property where your employer is operating his business is either his, or under his control as a lessee. So, as with any private property, owners may make the rules.

Second, your employer may make "no firearms" a condition of your employment, so be aware of anything you sign, or may have already signed, for an employer or prospective employer.

Your employer may extend the prohibition to any parking lots or adjoining property under his control. If you have a contract, and you have agreed to its conditions of employment, your employer can even dictate that you not have firearms *off company property* while you are working. Having a gun when your employer has forbidden it is not a crime, unless he has told you to leave the property and you remain. However, it may be cause for termination.

What about "public" employers?

The Oregon Appeals Court has ruled, in the case of *Jane Doe vs Medford School District,* that state agencies *may* make "no firearms" a condition of employment even though they are state agencies and Oregon's preemption law says that only the legislative assembly may make rules restricting the carrying of firearms by license holders.

Jane Doe was a teacher with a concealed handgun license who wanted to be able to carry her self defense tool to work. Her principal threatened her with both arrest and termination. (Of course, even if she took a gun to school, she would not be committing a crime.) She sued and the Oregon Firearms Educational Foundation paid her legal expenses. As stated, we lost. Keep in mind however, that the Medford School District never argued that their rule could apply to others on their property, only employees.

Doe was fearful of being unarmed, in part, because of concerns about her ex-husband. During the litigation we were constantly asked by the press what possible reason a teacher would ever have to carry a gun to school, implying that it was an inexcusable and dangerous idea. On Friday, February 26th 2010, Jennifer Paulson, a teacher at Birney Elementary School in Tacoma Washington, was gunned down by a stalker who had been harassing her for years. Her school also had a policy forbidding her from protecting herself.

Oregon law does not prohibit firearms on the campuses of state colleges and universities. However most have rules forbidding it. At the time this book went to print, the Oregon Firearms Educational Foundation was suing the Oregon University System to overturn these rules. The OUS applies these rules to everybody, not just students and employees, and as such, we maintain that they are not lawful.

The Oregon statute dealing with trespassing with a firearm, ORS 164.265 reads as follows:

Criminal trespass while in possession of firearm. (1) A person commits the crime of criminal trespass while in possession of a firearm who, while in possession of a firearm, enters or remains unlawfully in or upon premises.

(2) Criminal trespass while in possession of a firearm is a Class A misdemeanor. [1979 c.603 §2]

Preemption

Now you know how state law spells out where you may and may not carry a gun. At this point I need to discuss Oregon's "preemption" statute and how it has a major effect on this subject.

ORS 166.170 very clearly states:

"Except as expressly authorized by state statute, the authority to regulate in any matter whatsoever the sale, acquisition, transfer, ownership, possession, storage, transportation or use of firearms or any element relating to firearms and components thereof, including ammunition, is vested solely in the Legislative Assembly."

This seems to be pretty unambiguous. Only the Oregon Legislature can regulate guns. But there are some big "buts" here. Those "buts" appear in ORS 166. 171, 166.172 and 166.173.

166.171 allows counties to restrict where firearms may be discharged.

166.172 allows cities to restrict where firearms may be discharged, and....

166.273 allows cities and counties to "regulate possession of loaded firearms in public places." This is the big one.

Ultimately, what it means, is that although no *state* law prohibits non-licensees from openly carrying a loaded handgun, localities *may* restrict such carry. And some places do. For example, open carry is illegal for non license-holders in the City of Salem.

It is very important to know, that as noted above, in spite of the very clear language of the law, localities and agencies around the state often attempt to impose their own rules on gun owners, even when they are expressly forbidden from doing so.

In 2001, the city of Portland decided that to avoid the riots of the previous year, they would hold a "free" public New Year's party.

The party was paid for by taxpayers and held in a public square in downtown Portland.

The City announced that no weapons would be permitted within the fenced-in area where the "party" was being held. This applied to persons with concealed handgun licenses.

The policy was a clear violation of the law. Portland had no authority to impose this rule. The Oregon Firearms Educational Foundation went to court to seek a restraining order against the City on New Year's Eve with this author as plaintiff.

The Mayor of Portland, Vera Katz, hysterically overreacting as usual, announced that if we were issued the restraining order, she would order the event shut down!

A Multnomah County Judge carefully considered our request. He noted that the law did not allow the City to impose its own rules. Then he ruled that the event was a "private party" and as such was exempt from the law.

So, a publicly-funded event, on public property, advertised as a "City" sponsored function on the City's own website, morphed, through the magic of inventive courtroom procedure, into a "private" party.

Of course, the only people who could be excluded from the party were those who had gone through the expense and inconvenience of complying with the law and getting handgun licenses. Everyone else (even the previous year's rioters) was welcome.

OFEF filed a lawsuit against the city and about a year later, just before the next New Year's party, another Multnomah County Judge ruled that it wasn't really the City of Portland that sponsored the party, it was the "city" like a kind of abstract collection of communities, like a, well kind of like a...village!

(Remember that next time you get a water bill from an abstract collection of communities.)

The City did, however, rescind the illegal policy and has not attempted to enforce it since. A city attorney left a message for OFEF's lawyers saying gun owners were "evil and insane" but would be admitted to the festivities with their lawfully owned and carried handguns.

A later Appeals Court decision concluded that there were two issues:

1) Could persons having a private party on city property make up their own rules?

and

2) Was this a private party?

Obviously, our entire case rested on the fact that this was indeed a public event and as such, no rules against licensed concealed carry could be enacted. The court decided that yes, a private event could have anti-gun rules, but the City could not. As to the matter of whether or not it was a private party, well, they decided to just forget about that pesky detail, and ignore the question altogether. After all, the party was over.

Unfortunately, there is no central location where you can learn what the rules are for any place you may be in the state. And of course, these rules are not posted like speed limit signs when you drive into town, so you are largely on your own.

Virtually no legal restrictions on carry apply to persons with concealed handgun licenses, whether they are carrying openly or concealed. That includes schools. The exceptions, as noted above are, of course, court and federal facilities, where even license holders are forbidden from carrying guns.

I will deal with the concealed handgun licenses in the next chapter.

Chapter 5

Concealed Handgun Licenses

Oregon is a "shall issue" state. That means that unlike other places where your rights exist only with the approval of some bureaucrat, in Oregon, your "rights" exist as long as you have complied with a set of rules created by a whole collection of bureaucrats.

Oregon law says if you meet a certain set of criteria, the concealed handgun license must be issued.

Until 1989, county sheriffs had complete discretion over issuing or denying licenses. As you can imagine, in some counties, getting a concealed handgun license was virtually impossible. As with many other states, issuance was determined by your celebrity status or your relationship to the police bosses.

In 1989, the Oregon law was changed, and a uniform set of standards was enacted to determine eligibility. In the past, after the law changed, there were many sheriffs that were resistant to issuing CHLs and placed all kinds of roadblocks in the way. By and large, these issues seem to be a thing of the past and in many cases you can get an application from your county sheriff online. (There are still some county sheriffs that do not have websites however.) What follow are the requirements for CHL applicants:

1)   In order to apply for a concealed handgun license, you must be at least 21 years of age.

2) You must be either:
A) a US citizen or,
B) a legal resident alien who has declared in writing to the Immigration and Naturalization Service that you intend to become a US Citizen. There is no mandatory length of residency in the county for applicants who are US citizens. Aliens must have resided in the county for six months. Although noted nowhere in statute, many sheriffs are now requiring proof of citizenship for US citizens at the

time of application. (Some sheriffs have mistakenly applied the 6 month minimum residency requirement to citizens. This is not what the law requires.)

3)   You must not be a person required to register as a sex offender.

4)   You must not have been dishonorably discharged from the military.

5)   You must not have convictions involving controlled substances. (See more details below.)

6)   Your application needs to be made in the county in which you reside. The only exception to this rule is for applicants who live outside the state. I'll get to the rules for non-residents later.

7)   You must demonstrate competence with a handgun by having completed a class in firearms safety in which handgun safety was a "component" of that class or by one of several alternatives. (See more details below.)

The rules determining what qualified as "residency" changed in 2007. The new rules allow CHLs for an applicant that :

(a) Has a current Oregon driver license issued to the person showing a residence address in the county;
(b) Is registered to vote in the county and has a memorandum card issued to the person under ORS 247.181 showing a residence address in the county;
(c) Has documentation showing that the person currently leases or owns real property in the county; or
(d) Has documentation showing that the person filed an Oregon tax return for the most recent tax year showing a residence address in the county.

In some respects the requirements have become less stringent. Now merely owning or leasing property in the county qualifies you for a concealed handgun license. Previously the law required that you have a "principal residence" there.

The restrictions on people who have had convictions involving controlled substances were the result of efforts on the part of the Oregon Sheriffs to restrict handgun licenses in 2007. A quick look at the law can be very confusing. Here is what the law actually says defining a person who may apply for a concealed handgun license:

Has not been convicted of an offense involving controlled substances or participated in a court-supervised drug diversion program, except this disability does not operate to exclude a person if:

(A) The person has been convicted only once of violating ORS 475.864 (3) and has not completed a court-supervised drug diversion program under ORS 135.907; or

(B) The person has completed a court-supervised drug diversion program under ORS 135.907 and has not been convicted of violating ORS 475.864 (3);

What this means is that the prohibition on CHLs that would apply to persons with drug convictions, DOES NOT apply to a person with only one conviction for a small amount of marijuana. The language discussing "court supervised diversion programs" means that a person who completed a diversion program would be treated the same as a person with a single conviction of a small amount of marijuana. So, if you completed a diversion program and then were convicted of a second marijuana possession charge, that would be treated the same as two convictions and you would be prohibited from getting a CHL.

As mentioned earlier, you need to "demonstrate competency" with a handgun. Oregon law specifies what classes qualify. ORS 166.291 defines acceptable classes.

(A) Completion of any hunter education or hunter safety course approved by the State Department of Fish and Wildlife or a similar agency of another state if handgun safety was a component of the course;

(B) Completion of any National Rifle Association firearms safety or training course if handgun safety was a component of the course;

(C) Completion of any firearms safety or training course or class available to the general public offered by law enforcement, community college, or private or public institution or organization or firearms training school utilizing instructors certified by the National Rifle Association or a law enforcement agency if handgun safety was a component of the course;

(D) Completion of any law enforcement firearms safety or training course or class offered for security guards, investigators, reserve law enforcement officers or any other law enforcement officers if handgun safety was a component of the course;

(E) Presents evidence of equivalent experience with a handgun through participation in organized shooting competition or military service;

(F) Is licensed or has been licensed to carry a firearm in this state, unless the license has been revoked; or

(G) Completion of any firearms training or safety course or class conducted by a firearms instructor certified by a law enforcement agency or the National Rifle Association if handgun safety was a component of the course;

Note, your class does *not* have to be a regular NRA class. If the instructor is a certified NRA instructor, and handgun safety was included, your class qualifies.

As you can see, evidence of handgun training in the military also qualifies. However, be aware that many sheriffs will not accept a DD214 (the military issued document indicating firearms training) unless it specifically notes handgun training. If it says "small arms" training it will often be rejected.

Oregon law requires that "handgun safety" be a "component" of the class you take. It does not specify how long the class must be or how the class must be taught. It does not require range time. The instruction may be entirely of the "classroom" variety. Once you receive a certificate of training, there is no "expiration" date for using it to get a CHL and your class can be taken anywhere, you don't have to take it in Oregon.

Obviously, if you plan to carry a gun, it would be wise to get as much training as you can. Oregon has several excellent gun schools, and if you have an opportunity to attend any of them, your skills and knowledge will be greatly enhanced. But beyond the obvious benefits of being a better and safer shooter, you will have established that you are a responsible person who has done all he can to learn as much as possible about safe and effective firearms handling. This fact may serve you well in court someday.

The other requirements for obtaining a CHL are included in ORS 166.291. They require that the applicant:

(g) Has never been convicted of a felony or found guilty, except for insanity under ORS 161.295, of a felony;

(h) Has not been convicted of a misdemeanor or found guilty, except for insanity under ORS 161.295, of a misdemeanor within the four years prior to the application;

(i) Has not been committed to the Oregon Health Authority under ORS 426.130;

(j) Has not been found to be mentally ill and is not subject to an order under ORS 426.130 that the person be prohibited from purchasing or possessing a firearm as a result of that mental illness;

(k) Has been discharged from the jurisdiction of the juvenile court for more than four years if, while a minor, the person was found to be within the jurisdiction of the juvenile court for having committed an act that, if committed by an adult, would constitute a felony or a misdemeanor involving violence, as defined in ORS 166.470;

The short version of this is: no prior felonies, no misdemeanors within the last 4 years and no history of mental illness. Subsection "m" deals with persons who are the subject of certain kinds of restraining orders. It reads:

(m) Is not subject to a citation issued under ORS 163.735 or an order issued under ORS 30.866, 107.700 to 107.735 or 163.738;

The referenced sections deal with stalking, "family abuse" and restraining orders. Please be aware, there are other types of orders that are not listed in this section of the law. If you are denied or face a revocation because of a restraining order, it is important that you are aware what section of the law it was issued under.

CHLs are valid for four years. The fees for a CHL are $50.00 to the county sheriff and $15.00 to the State Police for fingerprinting. Renewals are $50.00 and, like applications, must be done in person unless you are an active duty member of the military, specifically if the renewer:

(A) Is an active member of the Armed Forces of the United States, the National Guard of the United States or the Oregon National Guard; and

(B) Submits with the application proof of the licensee's military orders and a copy of the licensee's military identification.

These people may renew by mail. As you might expect, there are continuing efforts to raise the fees for CHLs.

When you make your application, you will be photographed and fingerprinted. The sheriff will conduct a background check and you will be required to furnish two references. You might be asked to provide references within the county in which you are applying. However, that restriction is not authorized by law. Your references may come from outside the county or even the state.

The courts have found that the sheriffs may ask for information that is not required by statute. For example, they can ask who your employer is, or who your last three employers were. Based on Langlotz v. Noelle, there seem to be few things they cannot ask you. For non-resident licenses, it is very common for sheriffs to require the applicant to provide proof from their home states that they have not been found to be mentally ill. The process for doing this varies from state to state, but essentially comes down to you asking some bureaucrat to document that you're not crazy. Oregon residents need not provide similar documentation.

Oregon law requires that your CHL be issued, or you receive a reason for denial, within 45 days. (The law just says "days" not "business days.") Sometimes sheriffs take longer, but they are statutorily required to keep to the 45 day limit. If the license is not granted within 45 days, the applicant may seek relief under the same statute that would be used to contest a denial or revocation. 166.293 reads:

"If no decision is issued within 45 days, the person may seek review under the procedures in subsection (5) of this section."

Subsection 5 reads as follows:

(1) "A person denied a concealed handgun license or whose license is revoked or not renewed under ORS 166.291 to 166.295 may petition the circuit court in the petitioner's county of residence to review the denial, non-renewal or revocation. The petition must be filed within 30 days after the receipt of the notice of denial or revocation."

Your license is good for 4 years. The sheriff has NO obligation to send you a renewal notice. In fact, some counties sent out notices for years and then simply stopped without warning license holders. People who became accustomed to receiving notices suddenly found themselves in violation when their licenses expired without their knowledge. If your license is expired and you are carrying concealed, you are committing a Class A misdemeanor under ORS 166.250.

Whatever the policy of your sheriff, be aware that it can change without notice. Be sure to make note of the expiration date of your CHL. Some sheriffs are all too eager to revoke licenses. I'll deal with revocations in the next chapter.

Some have asked about getting a CHL if they have a medical marijuana card. There have been several cases where CHLs were returned by the courts after being revoked because the license holder had a medical marijuana card. The law says you cannot get a CHL if you have been "convicted of an offense involving controlled substances." It does *not* address medical marijuana cards. Many sheriffs will not issue a CHL to a person who they believe has "admitted" to using marijuana because those people are forbidden by federal law from owning firearms, but look for this unresolved issued to be litigated in the future.

Many sheriffs now have, as part of their applications, a requirement that you list the types and makes of guns you already own. These questions, on the applications I have seen, are directed towards anyone who answers "yes" to the questions about narcotics use. At this time there has been no ruling on the legality of these inquires. And you might wonder what purpose they serve.

Here is an explanation given to us by one Sheriff's office. According to the Sheriff of one southern Oregon county, persons who use narcotics are forbidden from owning guns by the Federal Government, but Federal laws only control firearms that have moved in interstate transport. The purpose of asking what type and brand of firearm a drug user already owns is to determine if, in fact, the guns they own "moved in interstate transport" and are thus unlawful to own. At this time we have been unable to learn exactly what the sheriffs do if they get an application from someone who admits to using drugs and also admits to having firearms.

Please note, many license holders are under the impression that they are required to immediately present a CHL to a police officer if they are pulled over for a traffic violation. There are even instructors who are telling their students that this is required. No such law exists in Oregon.

You have no obligation to volunteer your license to a police officer when you are pulled over. He will know that you have a CHL as soon as he runs your driver's license. Be aware that many police do not know the law and will tell you that you *must* offer this information. This is not true.

If you choose to offer your license voluntarily, be advised that there is no guarantee that this will be considered a friendly gesture by the officer in question. Use your common sense and instincts in this kind of circumstance.

Some people believe that possession of a CHL will allow you to bypass background checks on guns purchased from Federally licensed dealers. This is not true. All background checks still apply.

Non-Resident Licenses

Oregon allows non-residents to apply for a CHL if they meet all the other requirements and live in an adjoining state. However, in the case of non-residents, the sheriffs have complete discretion to deny a license for no cause. Furthermore, non- resident applicants must "have a compelling business interest or other legitimate demonstrated need."

It is worth noting that the law does *not* require that your "compelling business interest" be in the county in which you apply, only that it be in Oregon. Some counties have misinterpreted this part of the law. Whether they have done this deliberately or through ignorance is anyone's guess.

"Legitimate demonstrated need" can be as simple as "self defense" and some sheriffs have issued based on that alone. Other sheriffs have a blanket policy of not issuing under any circumstances.

Non-residents may apply in any county. But keep in mind, if you do find a friendly sheriff willing to issue a license, you'll have to go to that county to turn in the application. At least one sheriff has expressed interest in issuing non-resident CHLs at events like gun shows outside the state. I hope he is successful.

Issuance of CHLs for non-residents has been erratic and unpredictable. Some sheriffs have been quite willing to issue. Some, as noted, have almost always refused. Some have issued for a while and then stopped.

There is no pattern that I've been able to determine and sometimes non-resident CHLs are issued by sheriffs who are notoriously anti-gun.

Other States' Licenses

At this time Oregon recognizes no other states' licenses. At one time, Oregon law allowed the State Police to recognize other states' licenses if they felt that the issuing requirements were "substantially similar" to Oregon's.

In their infinite wisdom, the State Police decided that *no* other state met their lofty standards. In the mid '90s, with the approval of the geniuses in the establishment gun lobby, that law was changed to not even allow the *possibility* of accepting other states' licenses. The reasoning of the "gun lobby" at the time was that since the police were not accepting them anyway, why bother allowing it to be a possibility? (This was, of course, prior to the establishment of the Oregon Firearms Federation.) There are ongoing efforts to change Oregon's law to allow for recognition of other states' licenses.

Chapter 6

Dealing With Denials And Revocations

Prior to 2003, Oregon law pretty much allowed a license to be revoked for any of the same reasons that an initial application could be denied. In the 2003 legislative session a "housekeeping bill" passed nearly unanimously in both houses. When that happens you can bet it's because no one read it.

The bill in question, SB 81, made a small but important change in the gun law.

In section 166.293 (3) (a) one word and one number were changed. The section in question then read :

(3)(a) Any act or condition that would prevent the issuance of a license under ORS 166.291 and 166.292 is cause for revoking a concealed handgun license.

Previously, the law allowed a revocation for any act or condition that would prevent issuance under ORS *166.291 through 166.293.*

When 166.293 was removed from the reasons for a revocation, a sheriff could no longer revoke for any reason that was not included in 166.291 or 166.292. So,the following section no longer applied for revocations:

(2) Notwithstanding ORS 166.291 (1), and subject to review as provided in subsection (5) of this section, a sheriff may deny a concealed handgun license if the sheriff has reasonable grounds to believe that the applicant has been or is reasonably likely to be a danger to self or others, or to the community at large, as a result of the applicant's mental or psychological state, as demonstrated by past pattern of behavior or participation in incidents involving unlawful violence or threats of unlawful violence.

This meant that a sheriff's belief that a license holder was a "danger to self or others" no longer qualified as a reason for revocation, although it still could be a reason to deny a license in the first place.

In the case of Bates vs. Gordon, the Sheriff of Washington County had revoked a concealed handgun license because, in his estimation, the license holder (Bates) was a "danger" to others. The Oregon Appeals Court decided that the Oregon Legislature, through SB 81, had eliminated this as a valid reason for a revocation. As it turns out, the plaintiff in this case, Thomas Bates, wound up losing his CHL for unrelated reasons, but the courts found that his license could not be revoked because the sheriff thought he was a "danger to himself or others."

As you might expect, the Oregon legislature was beside itself. On December 14th, 2005 in an interim joint meeting of the House and Senate Judiciary Committee, the lawyers for the legislature presented a letter and their opinion on why they thought the courts got it wrong. They also informed the committee that they expected the Oregon Supreme Court to take up the matter and overturn the Appeals Court. In 2007 the Supreme Court did just that. They decided that the legislature, in fact, did not mean what it had said and reinstated the Sheriffs' ability to revoke for the same reasons that it denied. In May of 2007 the Legislature passed HB 2300 which formally changed the law back to the way it was before the initial mistake was made, thereby reinforcing the Supreme Court's decision and placing it into statute. You can now once again be revoked for the same reasons you can be denied.

If your concealed handgun license is revoked, you must be notified by the County Sheriff. The revocation does not take effect until you have received notification. That's an important point. It doesn't matter when the sheriff sent it, before the revocation is in effect, you must have received notice. (Noelle v. Young)

When that happens, what can you do? While this material is not meant to be legal advice, I hope this will help you to begin to get your license restored if the revocation was improper or not justified, or if you were denied a license improperly.

You must start immediately as the law doesn't give you much time to respond to this. If you can afford it, contact an attorney right away. Make sure you find one who has done this kind of work before. Your family probate attorney is simply not going to be good enough.

From here I will assume that you don't have the money for an attorney to do this job for you. In that case you will have to represent yourself, or go *pro se* ("pro-say").

ORS 166.293 (5) says,

"A person denied a concealed handgun license or whose license is revoked or not renewed under ORS 166.291 to 166.295 may petition the circuit court in the petitioner's county of residence to review the denial, non-renewal or revocation. The petition must be filed within 30 days after the receipt of the notice of denial or revocation."

As stated above, the words "receipt of the notice" here refers to when the letter was delivered, not sent. However, to be on the safe side, it might be wise to file your petition within 30 days of the date on the letter. So, within 30 days, you must file what is called a "petition" with the "circuit court in the petitioner's county of residence."

The petition is a relatively simple document (see the sample petition on page 139), but that only begins the process. I will discuss the step-by-step process of this filing below, but first I need to make several other things clear.

The reason why the 30 days may need to be carefully considered is that the statute provides that the hearing on the matter take place within 15 days of filing the petition.

ORS 166.293(8) says,

"Petitions filed under this section shall be heard and disposed of within 15 judicial days of filing or as soon as practicable thereafter."

If you are going *"pro se"*, 15 days is an awfully short time to prepare your case. This is especially true if you are unfamiliar with the law and how legal processes work.

You may wish to work on preparing your case through part, most, or even all of that 30 days before filing so that the 15 days is just more time in which to prepare. That time may be your best asset. In any event, you will need to spend time getting to know the part of Oregon law that is relevant to the revocation and the petition for review.

Take the time to read carefully through it before continuing with this. In the process of preparing your case, you will probably read these laws dozens of times. Specific words are very important in law, so you must not simply gloss over what you read. Your case is too important.

Making Your Case

You are going to have to make your case before a judge, so you will need to begin to think in legal terms. The court has standards within the law that require it to look at your case under specific terms.

ORS 166.293 (6) says:

(6) The judgment affirming or overturning the sheriff's decision shall be based on whether the petitioner meets the criteria that are used for issuance of a concealed handgun license and, if the petitioner was denied a concealed handgun license, whether the sheriff has reasonable grounds for denial under subsection (2) of this section. Whenever the petitioner has been previously sentenced for a crime under ORS 161.610 or for a crime of violence for which the person could have received a sentence of more than 10 years, the court shall grant relief only if the court finds that relief should be granted in the interest of justice.

This means that the court is supposed to be limited to considering your revocation based on whether you meet the criteria for getting your CHL in the first place. These criteria are listed in ORS 166.291 through 166.293. Your job now is to go back through each and every criterion listed in those three sections to make sure you are not in violation of any of them.

For instance, if you have recently been arrested or cited for a crime, the revocation will stand – at least until 30 days after the arrest if no charge is filed (ORS 166.293(4)) – or until you go to trial and are acquitted.

One of the things the sheriff is required to do in the revocation letter is specify "the grounds for the revocation" (ORS 166.293(3)(b)). While it will be important for you to concentrate on disproving the allegation in the letter, it is important to know that the sheriff may come into court claiming more grounds than were in the letter. You don't want to get caught off guard here. This is why it is important to gather evidence to show that you qualify under all the criteria in ORS 166.291 through 166.293.

At this point a warning is in order. Most judges tend to believe law enforcement personnel more than they deserve – and certainly more than they believe Joe Citizen. Remembering that will help you understand why you may need to have way more proof than you should really need that you qualify for the CHL under those statutes. Be ready for every eventuality.

Now we come to a very tricky section in the law.

ORS 166.293(2) says,

(2) Notwithstanding ORS 166.291 (1), and subject to review as provided in subsection (5) of this section, a sheriff may deny a concealed handgun license if the sheriff has reasonable grounds to believe that the applicant has been or is reasonably likely to be a danger to self or others, or to the community at large, as a result of the applicant's mental or psychological state or as demonstrated by the applicant's past pattern of behavior involving unlawful violence or threats of unlawful violence. (Emphasis added.)

You will note that the word "or" was highlighted in the text above. That word was not always a part of the law. It was added in 2007. Before that word was added, sheriffs had to show that a person was likely to be a danger to self or others by some demonstrated behavior. After "or" was added, the sheriff could deny or revoke a license based only on "mental or psychological state" with no incidents having occurred. There is no requirement that the sheriff have any credentials to determine your "mental or psychological state."

If you are revoked (or denied) based on this, you have every right to challenge the credentials of the sheriff to determine or analyze your "mental or psychological state." If the sheriff who denies or revokes you has no experience as a mental health professional, the court may very well find that he has overstepped his authority. Also note that the law calls for a "pattern of behavior" and "incidents" involving unlawful violence or threats of unlawful violence." It does not allow denial for a single event. But obviously, if you are denied or revoked based solely on the sheriff's perception of your mental state, that won't matter.

Beginning the Process

The first thing you will need to do officially is to file the petition with the circuit court within 30 days. (The statute does not say "business" days.) Bring your checkbook.

ORS 166.293(9) says,

"Filing fees for actions shall be as for any civil action filed in the court. If the petitioner prevails, the amount of the filing fee shall be paid by the respondent to the petitioner and may be incorporated into the court order."

In this state, those filing fees could be upwards of $200, so be prepared.

There may be an alternative, though. You will have to call or go to the court ahead of time to ask them about it. Depending on the county, you might be able to get your filing fees either waived altogether or at least deferred. This will involve a filling out a form declaring your income and assets, signed in front of a notary. If you qualify, you may not have to come up with the filing fee before filing.

As stated previously you must make out the petition in a similar fashion to the one reproduced in the Appendix, page 138.

Sign it and make half a dozen copies (just to be sure). Also make copies of the revocation letter to attach to the original and each copy. After making the copies, mark the original in the upper right-hand corner of the page with the word, ORIGINAL. Attach the revocation letter copies to the backs of each petition.

Take all of that to the filing desk at the county courthouse . When you file it, make sure that all the copies are stamped with the case number. The clerk will keep the original and as many copies as the court requires. Put the remaining copies in your own file.

Ask the clerk if you are responsible to serve the sheriff's office. If so, take a copy to the sheriff's office and ask the receptionist if she is allowed to "receive process" for the sheriff. If so, give it to the receptionist. If not, ask to whom you should give it and follow those instructions. Include a "certificate of service" like the one on page 140.

That done, the 15 days should commence. The court should contact you about when they will schedule the hearing.

Going to Court

When you finally go to court, you want to be fully prepared.

Any document you plan to use in your case should be marked and numbered – "Petitioner's Exhibit 1, 2, 3", etc.

You should have three copies of each – one is for you, one is for the court, and the last one is for your opponent.

Organize your documents so that you can find them quickly when you are in court.

If you are calling witnesses, make sure they are there on time, dressed presentably (as you should also be), and fully aware of the kinds of questions you will have for them.

In a loose-leaf binder, you should have a list of questions you want to make sure you ask your witnesses – so you don't forget. (It helps to put a small check mark next to a question once you have gotten your answer.) However, don't be a slave to the list. If you think of more questions that are pertinent while you are going though the list, ask them.

Don't be in a hurry. Don't get mad if the sheriff lies. Just remember, your main objective is not to prove people are lying or misunderstanding, but that you fully qualify for a CHL and that there is no "reasonable grounds" objective reason to think you are a danger to anyone.

Courtroom etiquette calls for you to stand every time you address the judge and address him as "Your Honor."

If your opponent is speaking, but there is something he says to which you need to respond, rise slowly so the court will know you need to speak further and wait until the judge tells you to proceed. Pay close attention to the comments made by the state's counsel for anything that falls outside of the qualifications for a CHL and be sure to object if he does.

Conclusion

Pro se defense is a daunting task. If you have never been to court before, it is even more so. However, with attention to presenting a clear and detailed defense of your right to have your CHL back, you could prevail. Some judges are impressed with meeting level-headed, competent people in their courts who are not "hiding behind attorneys," and that could work in your favor.

"No citizen shall be debarred the use of arms within his own lands."

—Thomas Jefferson

Chapter 7

Guns And Deadly Force

The use of deadly force is a dangerously complicated area of law. It is tremendously subjective. No two juries will come to the same conclusion about its justification, and there are plenty of people who would love nothing more than to hang another scalp on their wall by convicting a gun owner of a crime because he used a firearm in defense of himself or another person. In fact, I know of quite a few cases where gun owners were convicted of crimes simply because they had a gun in their possession but had done nothing else wrong.

Oregon does not have a statute dealing with "brandishing." By this I mean that there is no law that makes it illegal to show a gun, or allow it to be seen. However, it is a crime in Oregon to point a firearm at another person.

ORS 166.190 states the following:

"Pointing firearm at another; courts having jurisdiction over offense. Any person over the age of 12 years who, with or without malice, purposely points or aims any loaded or empty pistol, gun, revolver or other firearm, at or toward any other person within range of the firearm, except in self-defense, shall be fined upon conviction in any sum not less than $10 nor more than $500, or be imprisoned in the county jail not less than 10 days nor more than six months, or both. Justice courts have jurisdiction concurrent with the circuit court of the trial of violations of this section. When any person is charged before a justice court with violation of this section, the court shall, upon motion of the district attorney, at any time before trial, act as a committing magistrate, and if probable cause be established, hold such person to the grand jury. [Formerly 163.320]"

Further more, Oregon has a few other statutes that are commonly used against gun owners who have drawn guns in self defense. One is the "menacing" statute:

163.190 Menacing. (1) A person commits the crime of menacing if by word or conduct the person intentionally attempts to place another person in fear of imminent serious physical injury.

(2) Menacing is a Class A misdemeanor. [1971 c.743 §95]

Another is "disorderly conduct"

166.025 Disorderly conduct in the second degree. (1) A person commits the crime of disorderly conduct in the second degree if, with intent to cause public inconvenience, annoyance or alarm, or recklessly creating a risk thereof, the person:

(a) Engages in fighting or in violent, tumultuous or threatening behavior;

(b) Makes unreasonable noise;

(c) Disturbs any lawful assembly of persons without lawful authority;

(d) Obstructs vehicular or pedestrian traffic on a public way;

(e) Congregates with other persons in a public place and refuses to comply with a lawful order of the police to disperse;

(f) Initiates or circulates a report, knowing it to be false, concerning an alleged or impending fire, explosion, crime, catastrophe or other emergency; or

(g) Creates a hazardous or physically offensive condition by any act which the person is not licensed or privileged to do.

(2) Disorderly conduct in the second degree is a Class B misdemeanor. [1971 c.743 §220; 1983 c.546 §5; 2001 c.104 §55; 2005 c.631 §1]

Because of the complexity of the laws surrounding the use of deadly force, I have simply reproduced them (page 118) with the warning that should you ever find yourself in a situation where you need to use it, having a lawyer you trust will become very, very important. It would also serve you well as a gun owner to take advantage of the very best training you can afford. As noted earlier, Oregon has some excellent training facilities. The use of force statutes follow the gun laws in the back of the book.

Afterword

Owning a firearm is the hallmark of a free person. In Oregon, as in most of the rest of the USA, it's become a privilege reserved for those willing to submit themselves to a dizzying array of redundant and counterproductive regulations. It should not be this way. But the fact remains, if you choose to own a gun for defense of yourself and others, you'd better know the rules. Far too few people do.

Since 1998, the Oregon Firearms Federation has worked aggressively to protect the rights of gun owners in Oregon. But every gun owner has his own part to play.

Being a thoughtful and safe gun owner is only the most obvious of your responsibilities. Knowing as much as you can about the law is equally important.

This book contains all of Oregon's gun laws. These laws are also available to anyone online, as are Federal laws. The complete collection of BATFE rules (Bureau of Alcohol,Tobacco, Firearms and Explosives) can be downloaded from OFF's website as well as the BATFE's site.

http://www.atf.gov/publications/download/p/atf-p-5300-4.pdf

It's lengthy, but you should have it.

As I have pointed out, it's a mistake to think that the police or judges or even your own attorney will know the law. You owe it to yourself to learn as much about it as you can.

As I said before, knowledge is power. Stay safe and free.

"Who are the militia? They consist now of the whole people"

—George Mason "Father of the Bill of Rights"
Delegate to the Constitutional Convention

Appendix

Oregon's Revised Statutes

POSSESSION AND USE OF WEAPONS

166.180 Negligently wounding another. Any person who, as a result of failure to use ordinary care under the circumstances, wounds any other person with a bullet or shot from any firearm, or with an arrow from any bow, shall be punished by imprisonment in the county jail for a period not to exceed six months, or by a fine not to exceed $500, or both. In addition, any person so convicted shall forfeit any license to hunt, obtained under the laws of this state, and shall be ineligible to obtain a license to hunt for a period of 10 years following the date of conviction. [Formerly 163.310]

166.190 Pointing firearm at another; courts having jurisdiction over offense. Any person over the age of 12 years who, with or without malice, purposely points or aims any loaded or empty pistol, gun, revolver or other firearm, at or toward any other person within range of the firearm, except in self-defense, shall be fined upon conviction in any sum not less than $10 nor more than $500, or be imprisoned in the county jail not less than 10 days nor more than six months, or both. Justice courts have jurisdiction concurrent with the circuit court of the trial of violations of this section. When any person is charged before a justice court with violation of this section, the court shall, upon motion of the district attorney, at any time before trial, act as a committing magistrate, and if probable cause be established, hold such person to the grand jury. [Formerly 163.320]

166.210 Definitions. As used in ORS 166.250 to 166.270, 166.291 to 166.295 and 166.410 to 166.470
    (1) "Antique firearm" means:
        (a) Any firearm, including any firearm with a matchlock, flintlock, percussion cap or similar type of ignition system, manufactured in or before 1898; and

59

(b) Any replica of any firearm described in paragraph (a) of this subsection if the replica:

(A) Is not designed or redesigned for using rimfire or conventional centerfire fixed ammunition; or

(B) Uses rimfire or conventional centerfire fixed ammunition that is no longer manufactured in the United States and that is not readily available in the ordinary channels of commercial trade.

(2) "Corrections officer" has the meaning given that term in ORS 181.610.

(3) "Firearm" means a weapon, by whatever name known, which is designed to expel a projectile by the action of powder.

(4) "Firearms silencer" means any device for silencing, muffling or diminishing the report of a firearm.

(5) "Handgun" means any pistol or revolver using a fixed cartridge containing a propellant charge, primer and projectile, and designed to be aimed or fired otherwise than from the shoulder.

(6) "Machine gun" means a weapon of any description by whatever name known, loaded or unloaded, which is designed or modified to allow two or more shots to be fired by a single

(7) "Minor" means a person under 18 years of age.

(8) "Offense" has the meaning given that term in ORS 161.505.

(9) "Parole and probation officer" has the meaning given that term in ORS 181.610.

(10) "Peace officer" has the meaning given that term in ORS 133.005.

(11) "Short-barreled rifle" means a rifle having one or more barrels less than 16 inches in length and any weapon made from a rifle if the weapon has an overall length of less than 26 inches.

(12) "Short-barreled shotgun" means a shotgun having one or more barrels less than 18 inches in length and any weapon made from a shotgun if the weapon has an overall length of less than 26 inches. [Amended by 1977 c.769 §1; 1979 c.779 §3; 1989 c.839 §1; 1993 c.735 §14; 1995 c.670 §3; 1999 c.1040 §2; 2001 c.666 §§32,44; 2003 c.614 §7; 2007 c.368 §1; 2009 c.610 §4]

166.220 Unlawful use of weapon. (1) A person commits the crime of unlawful use of a weapon if the person:

(a) Attempts to use unlawfully against another, or carries or possesses with intent to use unlawfully against another, any dangerous or deadly weapon as defined in ORS

161.015; or

(b) Intentionally discharges a firearm, blowgun, bow and arrow, crossbow or explosive device within the city limits of any city or within residential areas within urban growth boundaries at or in the direction of any person, building, structure or vehicle within the range of the weapon without having legal authority for such discharge.

(2) This section does not apply to:

(a) Police officers or military personnel in the lawful performance of their official duties;

(b) Persons lawfully defending life or property as provided in ORS 161.219;

(c) Persons discharging firearms, blowguns, bows and arrows, crossbows or explosive devices upon public or private shooting ranges, shooting galleries or other areas designated and built for the purpose of target shooting;

(d) Persons lawfully engaged in hunting in compliance with rules and regulations adopted by the State Department of Fish and Wildlife; or

(e) An employee of the United States Department of Agriculture, acting within the scope of employment, discharging a firearm in the course of the lawful taking of wildlife.

(3) Unlawful use of a weapon is a Class C felony. [Amended by 1975 c.700 §1; 1985 c.543 §1; 1991 c.797 §1; 2009 c.556 §5]

166.230 [Repealed by 1979 c.779 §7]

166.240 Carrying of concealed weapons. (1) Except as provided in subsection (2) of this section, any person who carries concealed upon the person any knife having a blade that projects or swings into position by force of a spring or by centrifugal force, any dirk, dagger, ice pick, slungshot, metal knuckles, or any similar instrument by the use of which injury could be inflicted upon the person or property of any other person, commits a Class B misdemeanor.

(2) Nothing in subsection (1) of this section applies to any peace officer as defined in ORS 133.005, whose duty it is to serve process or make arrests. Justice courts have concurrent jurisdiction to try any person charged with violating any of the provisions of subsection (1) of this section. [Amended by 1977 c.454 §1; 1985 c.543 §2; 1989 c.839 §21; 1999 c.1040 §15]

166.245 [1989 c.839 §38; repealed by 1995 s.s. c.1 §7]

166.250 Unlawful possession of firearms. (1) Except as otherwise provided in this section or ORS 166.260, 166.270, 166.274, 166.291, 166.292 or 166.410 to 166.470, a person commits the crime of unlawful possession of a firearm if the person knowingly:

(a) Carries any firearm concealed upon the person;

(b) Possesses a handgun that is concealed and readilyaccessible to the person within any vehicle; or

(c) Possesses a firearm and:

(A) Is under 18 years of age;

(B)(i) While a minor, was found to be within the jurisdiction of the juvenile court for having committed an act which, if committed by an adult, would constitute a felony or a misdemeanor involving violence, as defined in ORS 166.470; and

(ii) Was discharged from the jurisdiction of the juvenile court within four years prior to being charged under this section;

(C) Has been convicted of a felony;

(D) Was committed to the Oregon Health Authority under ORS 426.130;

(E) Was found to be mentally ill and subject to an order under ORS 426.130 that the person be prohibited from purchasing or possessing a firearm as a result of that mental illness; or

(F) Has been found guilty except for insanity under ORS 161.295 of a felony.

(2) This section does not prohibit:

(a) A minor, who is not otherwise prohibited under subsection (1)(c) of this section, from possessing a firearm:

(A) Other than a handgun, if the firearm was transferred to the minor by the minor's parent or guardian or by another person with the consent of the minor's parent or guardian; or

(B) Temporarily for hunting, target practice or any other lawful purpose; or

(b) Any citizen of the United States over the age of 18 years who resides in or is temporarily sojourning within this state, and who is not within the excepted classes prescribed by ORS 166.270 and subsection (1) of this section, from owning, possessing or keeping within the person's place of residence or place of business any handgun, and no permit or license to purchase, own, possess or keep any such firearm at the person's place of residence or place of business is required of any such citizen. As used in this subsection, "residence" includes a recreational vessel or recreational vehicle while used, for whatever period of time, as residential quarters.

(3) Firearms carried openly in belt holsters are not concealed within the meaning of this section.

(4)(a) Except as provided in paragraph (b) of this subsection, a handgun is readily accessible within the meaning of this section if the handgun is within the passenger compartment of the vehicle.

(b) If a vehicle has no storage location that is outside the passenger compartment of the vehicle, a handgun is not readily accessible within the meaning of this section if:

(A) The handgun is stored in a closed and locked glove compartment, center console or other container; and

(B) The key is not inserted into the lock, if the glove compartment, center console or other container unlocks with a key.

(5) Unlawful possession of a firearm is a Class A misdemeanor.[Amended by 1979 c.779 §4; 1985 c.543 §3; 1989 c.839 §13; 1993 c.732 §1; 1993 c.735 §12; 1999 c.1040 §1; 2001 c.666 §§33,45; 2003 c.614 §8; 2009 c.499 §1; 2009 c.595 §112]

Note 1: The amendments to 166.250 by section 8a, chapter 826, Oregon Laws 2009, become operative on the date that the rule described in section 13 (1), chapter 826, Oregon Laws 2009, is adopted by the Psychiatric Security Review Board. See section 13, chapter 826, Oregon Laws 2009, as amended by section 22, chapter 826, Oregon Laws 2009 (Note 4 under 166.274). The text that is operative from the date of adoption of that rule until January 2, 2012, is set forth for the user's convenience.

166.250. (1) Except as otherwise provided in this section or ORS 166.260, 166.270, 166.274, 166.291, 166.292 or 166.410 to 166.470 or section 5, chapter 826, Oregon Laws 2009, a person commits the crime of unlawful possession of a firearm if the person knowingly:

(a) Carries any firearm concealed upon the person;

(b) Possesses a handgun that is concealed and readily accessible to the person within any vehicle; or

(c) Possesses a firearm and:

(A) Is under 18 years of age;

(B)(i) While a minor, was found to be within the jurisdiction of the juvenile court for having committed an act which, if committed by an adult, would constitute a felony or a misdemeanor involving violence, as defined in ORS 166.470; and

(ii) Was discharged from the jurisdiction of the juvenile court within four years prior to being charged under this section;

(C) Has been convicted of a felony;

(D) Was committed to the Oregon Health Authority under ORS 426.130;

(E) Was found to be mentally ill and subject to an order under ORS 426.130 that the person be prohibited from purchasing or possessing a firearm as a result of that mental illness; or

(F) Has been found guilty except for insanity under ORS 161.295 of a felony.

(2) This section does not prohibit:

(a) A minor, who is not otherwise prohibited under subsection (1)(c) of this section, from possessing a firearm:

(A) Other than a handgun, if the firearm was transferred to the minor by the minor's parent or guardian or by another person with the consent of the minor's parent or guardian; or

(B) Temporarily for hunting, target practice or any other lawful purpose; or

(b) Any citizen of the United States over the age of 18 years who resides in or is temporarily sojourning within this state, and who is not within the excepted classes prescribed by ORS 166.270 and subsection (1) of this section, from owning, possessing or keeping within the person's place of residence or place of business any handgun, and no permit or license to purchase, own, possess or keep any such firearm at the person's place of residence or place of business is required of any such citizen. As used in this subsection, "residence" includes a recreational vessel or recreational vehicle while used, for whatever period of time, as residential quarters.

(3) Firearms carried openly in belt holsters are not concealed within the meaning of this section.

(4)(a) Except as provided in paragraph (b) of this subsection, a handgun is readily accessible within the meaning of this section if the handgun is within the passenger compartment of the vehicle.

(b) If a vehicle has no storage location that is outside the passenger compartment of the vehicle, a handgun is not readily accessible within the meaning of this section if:

(A) The handgun is stored in a closed and locked glove compartment, center console or other container; and

(B) The key is not inserted into the lock, if the glove compartment, center console or other container unlocks with a key.

(5) Unlawful possession of a firearm is a Class A misdemeanor.

Note 2: The amendments to 166.250 by section 11a, chapter 826, Oregon Laws 2009, become operative January 2, 2012. See section 14, chapter 826, Oregon Laws 2009, as amended by section 23, chapter 826, Oregon Laws 2009. The text that is operative on and after January 2, 2012, is set forth for the user's convenience.

166.250. (1) Except as otherwise provided in this section or ORS 166.260, 166.270, 166.274, 166.291, 166.292 or 166.410 to 166.470, a person commits the crime of unlawful possession of a firearm if the person knowingly:

(a) Carries any firearm concealed upon the person;

(b) Possesses a handgun that is concealed and readily accessible to the person within any vehicle; or

(c) Possesses a firearm and:

(A) Is under 18 years of age;

(B)(i) While a minor, was found to be within the jurisdiction of the juvenile court for having committed an act which, if committed by an adult, would constitute a felony or a misdemeanor involving violence, as defined in ORS 166.470; and

(ii) Was discharged from the jurisdiction of the juvenile court within four years prior to being charged under this section;

(C) Has been convicted of a felony;

(D) Was committed to the Oregon Health Authority under ORS 426.130;

(E) Was found to be mentally ill and subject to an order under ORS 426.130 that the person be prohibited from purchasing or possessing a firearm as a result of that mental illness; or

(F) Has been found guilty except for insanity under ORS 161.295 of a felony.

(2) This section does not prohibit:

(a) A minor, who is not otherwise prohibited under subsection (1)(c) of this section, from possessing a firearm:

(A) Other than a handgun, if the firearm was transferred to the minor by the minor's parent or guardian or by another person with the consent of the minor's parent or guardian; or

(B) Temporarily for hunting, target practice or any other lawful purpose; or

(b) Any citizen of the United States over the age of 18 years who resides in or is temporarily sojourning within this state, and who is not within the excepted classes prescribed by ORS 166.270 and subsection (1) of this section, from owning, possessing or keeping within the person's place of residence or place of business any handgun, and no permit or license to purchase, own, possess or keep any such firearm at the person's place of residence or place of business is required of any such citizen. As used in this subsection, "residence" includes a recreational vessel or recreational vehicle while used, for whatever period of time, as residential quarters.

(3) Firearms carried openly in belt holsters are not concealed within the meaning of this section.

(4)(a) Except as provided in paragraph (b) of this subsection, a handgun is readily accessible within the meaning of this section if the handgun is within the passenger compartment of the vehicle.

(b) If a vehicle has no storage location that is outside the passenger compartment of the vehicle, a handgun is not readily accessible within the meaning of this section if:

(A) The handgun is stored in a closed and locked glove compartment, center console or other container; and

(B) The key is not inserted into the lock, if the glove compartment, center console or other container unlocks with a key.

(5) Unlawful possession of a firearm is a Class A misdemeanor.

166.260 Persons not affected by ORS 166.250. (1) ORS 166.250 does not apply to or affect:

(a) Sheriffs, constables, marshals, parole and probation officers, police officers, whether active or honorably retired, or other duly appointed peace officers.

(b) Any person summoned by any such officer to assist in making arrests or preserving the peace, while said person so summoned is actually engaged in assisting the officer.

(c) The possession or transportation by any merchant of unloaded firearms as merchandise.

(d) Active or reserve members of the Army, Navy, Air Force, Coast Guard or Marine Corps of the United States, or of the National Guard, when on duty.

(e) Organizations which are by law authorized to purchase or receive weapons described in ORS 166.250 from the United States, or from this state.

(f) Duly authorized military or civil organizations while parading, or the members thereof when going to and from the places of meeting of their organization.

(g) A corrections officer while transporting or accompanying an individual convicted of or arrested for an offense and confined in a place of incarceration or detention while outside the confines of the place of incarceration or detention.

(h) A person who is licensed under ORS 166.291 and 166.292 to carry a concealed handgun.

(2) It is an affirmative defense to a charge of violating ORS 166.250 (1)(c)(C) that the person has been granted relief from the disability under ORS 166.274.

(3) Except for persons who are otherwise prohibited from possessing a firearm under ORS 166.250 (1)(c) or 166.270, ORS 166.250 does not apply to or affect:

(a) Members of any club or organization, for the purpose of practicing shooting at targets upon the established target ranges, whether public or private, while such members are using any of the firearms referred to in ORS 166.250 upon such target ranges, or while going to and from such ranges.

(b) Licensed hunters or fishermen while engaged in hunting or fishing, or while going to or returning from a hunting or fishing expedition.

(4) The exceptions listed in subsection (1)(b) to (h) of this section constitute affirmative defenses to a charge of violating ORS 166.250. [Amended by 1977 c.207 §1; 1991 c.67 §36; 1993 c.735 §1; 1995 c.670 §2; 1999 c.1040 §3; 2009 c.316 §2; 2009 c.499 §4]

166.262 Limitation on peace officer's authority to arrest for violating ORS 166.250 or 166.370. A peace officer may not arrest or charge a person for violating ORS 166.250 (1)(a) or (b) or 166.370 (1) if the person has in the person's immediate possession a valid license to carry a firearm as provided in ORS 166.291 and 166.292. [1999 c.1040 §5]

166.263 Authority of parole and probation officer to carry firearm. When authorized by the officer's employer, a parole and probation officer, as defined in ORS 181.610, may carry a firearm while engaged in official duties if the officer has completed:
(1) A firearms training program recognized by the Board on Public Safety Standards and Training; and
(2) A psychological screening. [1995 c.670 §1]

166.270 Possession of weapons by certain felons. (1) Any person who has been convicted of a felony under the law of this state or any other state, or who has been convicted of a felony under the laws of the Government of the United States, who owns or has in the person's possession or under the person's custody or control any firearm commits the crime of felon in possession of a firearm.
(2) Any person who has been convicted of a felony under the law of this state or any other state, or who has been convicted of a felony under the laws of the Government of the United States, who owns or has in the person's possession or under the person's custody or control any instrument or weapon having a blade that projects or swings into position by force of a spring or by centrifugal force or any blackjack, slungshot, sandclub, sandbag, sap glove, metal knuckles or an Electro-Muscular Disruption Technology device as defined in ORS 165.540, or who carries a dirk, dagger or stiletto, commits the crime of felon in possession of a restricted weapon.
(3) For the purposes of this section, a person "has been convicted of a felony" if, at the time of conviction for an offense, that offense was a felony under the law of the jurisdiction in which it was committed. Such conviction shall not be deemed a conviction of a felony if:
(a) The court declared the conviction to be a misdemeanor at the time of judgment; or
(b) The offense was possession of marijuana and the conviction was prior to January 1, 1972.
(4) Subsection (1) of this section does not apply to any person who has been:
(a) Convicted of only one felony under the law of this state or any other state, or who has been convicted of only one felony under the laws of the United States, which felony did not involve criminal homicide, as defined in ORS 163.005, or the possession or use of a firearm or a weapon having a blade that projects or swings into position by force of a spring or by centrifugal force, and who has been

discharged from imprisonment, parole or probation for said offense for a period of 15 years prior to the date of alleged violation of subsection (1) of this section; or

(b) Granted relief from the disability under 18 U.S.C. 925(c) or ORS 166.274 or has had the person's record expunged under the laws of this state or equivalent laws of another jurisdiction.

(5) Felon in possession of a firearm is a Class C felony. Felon in possession of a restricted weapon is a Class A misdemeanor. [Amended by 1975 c.702 §1; 1985 c.543 §4; 1985 c.709 §2; 1987 c.853 §1; 1989 c.839 §4; 1993 c.735 §2; 1995 c.518 §1; 1999 c.1040 §16; 2003 c.14 §64; 2009 c.189 §1; 2009 c.499 §3]

166.272 Unlawful possession of machine guns, certain short-barreled firearms and firearms silencers. (1) A person commits the crime of unlawful possession of a machine gun, short-barreled rifle, short-barreled shotgun or firearms silencer if the person knowingly possesses any machine gun, short-barreled rifle, short-barreled shotgun or firearms silencer.

(2) Unlawful possession of a machine gun, short-barreled rifle, short-barreled shotgun or firearms silencer is a Class B felony.

(3) A peace officer may not arrest or charge a person for violating subsection (1) of this section if the person has in the person's immediate possession documentation showing that the machine gun, short-barreled rifle, short-barreled shotgun or firearms silencer is registered as required under federal law.

(4) It is an affirmative defense to a charge of violating subsection (1) of this section that the machine gun, short-barreled rifle, short-barreled shotgun or firearms silencer was registered as required under federal law. [1989 c.839 §13a; 1997 c.749 §8; 1997 c.798 §1]

166.274 Relief from prohibition against possessing or purchasing firearm. (1) A person barred from possessing a firearm under ORS 166.250 (1)(c)(A) to (E) or 166.270 or barred from purchasing a firearm under ORS 166.470 (1)(a) to (g) may file a petition for relief from the bar in:

(a) A justice court in the petitioner's county of residence that is reasonably accessible to the petitioner; or

(b) If no justice court is reasonably accessible, the circuit court.

(2) A person may apply once per calendar year for relief under the provisions of this section.

(3)(a) A person petitioning for relief under this section shall serve a copy of the petition on:
 (A) The city chief of police if the court in which the petition is filed is located in a city; or
 (B) The sheriff of the county in which the court is located.
(b) The copy of the petition shall be served on the chief of police or sheriff at the same time the petition is filed at the court.

(4)(a) When a petition is denied, the judge shall cause that information to be entered into the Department of State Police computerized criminal history files.

(b) When a petition is granted, the judge shall cause that information and a fingerprint card of the petitioner to be entered into the Department of State Police computerized criminal history files. If, after a petition is granted, the petitioner is arrested and convicted of a crime that would disqualify the petitioner from purchasing or possessing a firearm, the Department of State Police shall notify the court that granted relief under this section. The court shall review the order granting relief and determine whether to rescind the order. The Department of State Police may charge a reasonable fee, under ORS 192.440, for the entry and maintenance of information under this section.

(5) Notwithstanding the provisions of ORS 9.320, a corporation, the state or any city, county, district or other political subdivision or public corporation in this state, without appearance by attorney, may appear as a party to an action under this section.

(6) If the petitioner seeks relief from the bar on possessing or purchasing a firearm, relief shall be granted when the petitioner demonstrates, by clear and convincing evidence, that the petitioner does not pose a threat to the safety of the public or the petitioner.

(7) A person barred from possessing or purchasing a firearm because the person, while a minor, was found to be within the jurisdiction of the juvenile court for committing an act which, if committed by an adult, would have constituted a felony or a misdemeanor involving violence, is not eligible to petition for relief under this section until more than four years have passed since the person was discharged from the jurisdiction of the juvenile court.

(8) Petitions filed under this section shall be heard and disposed of within 15 judicial days of filing or as soon as is practicable thereafter, but not more than 30 days thereafter. The

judge shall then make findings and conclusions and issue a judgment based on the findings and conclusions in accordance with the requirements of law.

(9) Filing fees shall be as for any civil action filed in the court.

(10)(a) Initial appeals of petitions shall be heard de novo.

(b) Any party to a judgment under this subsection may appeal to the Court of Appeals in the same manner as for any other civil action.

(c) If the governmental entity files an appeal under this subsection and does not prevail, it shall be ordered to pay the attorney fees for the prevailing party. [1989 c.839 §11; 1991 c.67 §37; 1993 c.732 §§3,4; 1995 c.518 §2; 1995 c.658 §88; 2009 c.499 §2]

Note 1: The amendments to 166.274 by section 19, chapter 826, Oregon Laws 2009, become operative on the date that the rule described in section 13 (1), chapter 826, Oregon Laws 2009, is adopted by the Psychiatric Security Review Board. See section 13, chapter 826, Oregon Laws 2009, as amended by section 22, chapter 826, Oregon Laws 2009 (Note 4 under 166.274). The text that is operative from the date of adoption of that rule until January 2, 2012, is set forth for the user's convenience.

166.274. (1) A person barred from possessing or purchasing a firearm may file a petition for relief from the bar in accordance with subsection (2) of this section if:

(a) The person is barred from possessing a firearm under ORS 166.250 (1)(c)(A) to (C) or 166.270; or

(b) The person is barred from purchasing a firearm under ORS 166.470 (1)(a) to (d) or (g).

(2) A petition for relief described in this section must be filed in:

(a) A justice court in the petitioner's county of residence that is reasonably accessible to the petitioner; or

(b) If no justice court is reasonably accessible, the circuit court.

(3) A person may apply once per calendar year for relief under the provisions of this section.

(4)(a) A person petitioning for relief under this section shall serve a copy of the petition on:

(A) The city chief of police if the court in which the petition is filed is located in a city; or

(B) The sheriff of the county in which the court is located.

(b) The copy of the petition shall be served on the chief of police or sheriff at the same time the petition is filed at the court.

(5)(a) When a petition is denied, the judge shall cause that information to be entered into the Department of State Police computerized criminal history files.

(b) When a petition is granted, the judge shall cause that information and a fingerprint card of the petitioner to be entered into the Department of State Police computerized criminal history files. If, after a petition is granted, the petitioner is arrested and convicted of a crime that would disqualify the petitioner from purchasing or possessing a firearm, the Department of State Police shall notify the court that granted relief under this section. The court shall review the order granting relief and determine whether to rescind the order. The Department of State Police may charge a reasonable fee, under ORS 192.440, for the entry and maintenance of information under this section.

(6) Notwithstanding the provisions of ORS 9.320, a corporation, the state or any city, county, district or other political subdivision or public corporation in this state, without appearance by attorney, may appear as a party to an action under this section.

(7) If the petitioner seeks relief from the bar on possessing or purchasing a firearm, relief shall be granted when the petitioner demonstrates, by clear and convincing evidence, that the petitioner does not pose a threat to the safety of the public or the petitioner.

(8) A person barred from possessing or purchasing a firearm because the person, while a minor, was found to be within the jurisdiction of the juvenile court for committing an act which, if committed by an adult, would have constituted a felony or a misdemeanor involving violence, is not eligible to petition for relief under this section until more than four years have passed since the person was discharged from the jurisdiction of the juvenile court.

(9) Petitions filed under this section shall be heard and disposed of within 15 judicial days of filing or as soon as is practicable thereafter, but not more than 30 days thereafter. The judge shall then make findings and conclusions and issue a judgment based on the findings and conclusions in accordance with the requirements of law.

(10) Filing fees shall be as for any civil action filed in the court.

(11)(a) Initial appeals of petitions shall be heard de novo.

(b) Any party to a judgment under this subsection may appeal to the Court of Appeals in the same manner as for any other civil action.

(c) If the governmental entity files an appeal under this subsection and does not prevail, it shall be ordered to pay the attorney fees for the prevailing party.

Note 2: The amendments to 166.274 by section 20, chapter 826, Oregon Laws 2009, become operative January 2, 2012. See section 14, chapter 826, Oregon Laws 2009, as amended by section 23, chapter 826, Oregon Laws 2009. The text that is operative on and after January 2, 2012, is set forth for the user's convenience.

166.274. (1) A person barred from possessing a firearm under ORS 166.250 (1)(c)(A) to (E) or 166.270 or barred from purchasing a firearm under ORS 166.470 (1)(a) to (g) may file a petition for relief from the bar in:

(a) A justice court in the petitioner's county of residence that is reasonably accessible to the petitioner; or

(b) If no justice court is reasonably accessible, the circuit court.

(2) A person may apply once per calendar year for relief under the provisions of this section.

(3)(a) A person petitioning for relief under this section shall serve a copy of the petition on:

(A) The city chief of police if the court in which the petition is filed is located in a city; or

(B) The sheriff of the county in which the court is located.

(b) The copy of the petition shall be served on the chief of police or sheriff at the same time the petition is filed at the court.

(4)(a) When a petition is denied, the judge shall cause that information to be entered into the Department of State Police computerized criminal history files.

(b) When a petition is granted, the judge shall cause that information and a fingerprint card of the petitioner to be entered into the Department of State Police computerized criminal history files. If, after a petition is granted, the petitioner is arrested and convicted of a crime that would disqualify the petitioner from purchasing or possessing a firearm, the Department of State Police shall notify the court that granted relief under this section. The court shall review the order granting relief and determine whether to rescind the order. The Department of State Police may charge a reasonable fee, under ORS 192.440, for the entry and maintenance of information under this section.

(5) Notwithstanding the provisions of ORS 9.320, a corporation, the state or any city, county, district or other political subdivision or public corporation in this state, without appearance by attorney, may appear as a party to an action under this section.

(6) If the petitioner seeks relief from the bar on possessing or purchasing a firearm, relief shall be granted when the petitioner demonstrates, by clear and convincing evidence, that the petitioner does not pose a threat to the safety of the public or the petitioner.

(7) A person barred from possessing or purchasing a firearm because the person, while a minor, was found to be within the jurisdiction of the juvenile court for committing an act which, if committed by an adult, would have constituted a felony or a misdemeanor involving violence, is not eligible to petition for relief under this section until more than four years have passed since the person was discharged from the jurisdiction of the juvenile court.

(8) Petitions filed under this section shall be heard and disposed of within 15 judicial days of filing or as soon as is practicable thereafter, but not more than 30 days thereafter. The judge shall then make findings and conclusions and issue a judgment based on the findings and conclusions in accordance with the requirements of law.

(9) Filing fees shall be as for any civil action filed in the court.

(10)(a) Initial appeals of petitions shall be heard de novo.

(b) Any party to a judgment under this subsection may appeal to the Court of Appeals in the same manner as for any other civil action.

(c) If the governmental entity files an appeal under this subsection and does not prevail, it shall be ordered to pay the attorney fees for the prevailing party.

Note 3: Section 4 (22), chapter 659, Oregon Laws 2009, provides:
Sec. 4. (22) In addition to the fee provided for in ORS 166.274, for the period commencing October 1, 2009, and ending June 30, 2011, the clerk of the court shall collect a surcharge of $5 for the filing of a petition for relief under ORS 166.274. [2009 c.659 §4(22)]

Note 4: Sections 5, 13, 14 and 15, chapter 826, Oregon Laws 2009, provide:
Sec. 5. Relief from certain prohibitions against transporting, shipping, possessing or receiving firearm. (1) A person barred

from transporting, shipping, possessing or receiving a firearm may file a petition with the Psychiatric Security Review Board for relief from the bar if:

(a) The person is barred from possessing a firearm under ORS 166.250 (1)(c)(D) or (E);

(b) The person is barred from receiving a firearm under ORS 166.470 (1)(e) or (f); or

(c) The person is barred from possessing, receiving, shipping or transporting a firearm under 18 U.S.C. 922(d)(4) or (g)(4) as the result of a state mental health determination.

(2) The petitioner shall serve a copy of the petition on:

(a) The Department of Human Services and the Oregon Health Authority; and

(b) The district attorney in each county in which:

(A) The person was committed by a court to the Oregon Health Authority, or adjudicated by a court as mentally ill, under ORS 426.130;

(B) The person was committed by a court to the Department of Human Services, or adjudicated by a court as mentally retarded, under ORS 427.290;

(C) The person was found guilty except for insanity under ORS 161.295;

(D) The person was found responsible except for insanity under ORS 419C.411; or

(E) The person was found by a court to lack fitness to proceed under ORS 161.370.

(3) Following receipt of the petition, the board shall conduct a contested case hearing, make written findings of fact and conclusions of law on the issues before the board and issue a final order.

(4) The state and any person or entity described in subsection (2) of this section may appear and object to and present evidence relevant to the relief sought by the petitioner.

(5) The board shall grant the relief requested in the petition if the petitioner demonstrates, based on the petitioner's reputation, the petitioner's record, the circumstances surrounding the firearm disability and any other evidence in the record, that the petitioner will not be likely to act in a manner that is dangerous to public safety and that granting the relief would not be contrary to the public interest.

(6) If the board grants the relief requested in the petition, the board shall provide to the Department of State Police the minimum information necessary, as defined in section 1 of this 2009 Act [181.740], to enable the department to:

(a) Maintain the information and transmit the information to the federal government as required under federal law; and

(b) Maintain a record of the person's relief from the disqualification to possess or receive a firearm under ORS 166.250 (1)(c)(D) or (E) or 166.470 (1)(e) or (f).

(7) The petitioner may petition for judicial review of a final order of the board. The petition shall be filed in the circuit court of a county described in subsection (2)(b) of this section. The review shall be conducted de novo and without a jury.

(8) A petitioner may take an appeal from the circuit court to the Court of Appeals. Review by the Court of Appeals shall be conducted in accordance with ORS 183.500.

(9) A person may file a petition for relief under this section no more than once every two years.

(10) The board shall adopt procedural rules to carry out the provisions of this section.

(11) As used in this section, "state mental health determination" means:

(a) A finding by a court that a person lacks fitness to proceed under ORS 161.370;

(b) A finding that a person is guilty except for insanity of a crime under ORS 161.295 or responsible except for insanity of an act under ORS 419C.411 or any determination by the Psychiatric Security Review Board thereafter;

(c) A commitment by a court to the Oregon Health Authority, or an adjudication by a court that a person is mentally ill, under ORS 426.130; or

(d) A commitment by a court to the Department of Human Services, or an adjudication by a court that a person is mentally retarded, under ORS 427.290. [2009 c.826 §5; 2009 c.826 §§18,18a]

Sec. 13. (1) When the Psychiatric Security Review Board determines that the board has received a sufficient legislative appropriation or federal funding to carry out the provisions of section 5 of this 2009 Act, the board shall adopt a rule so indicating. The board shall notify Legislative Counsel upon adoption of the rule.

(2) Section 5 of this 2009 Act and the amendments to ORS 166.250, 166.274, 166.291 and 166.470 by sections 7, 8, 8a and 19 of this 2009 Act become operative on the date the rule described in subsection (1) of this section is adopted. [2009 c.826 §13; 2009 c.826 §22]

Sec. 14. (1) Sections 5 and 13 of this 2009 Act are repealed on January 2, 2012.
(2) The amendments to ORS 166.250, 166.274, 166.291 and 166.470 by sections 10, 11, 11a and 20 of this 2009 Act become operative on January 2, 2012. [2009 c.826 §14; 2009 c.826 §23]

Sec. 15. (1) The repeal of section 5 of this 2009 Act by section 14 of this 2009 Act does not affect any petition for relief filed pursuant to section 5 of this 2009 Act with the Psychiatric Security Review Board before January 2, 2012. Any proceeding commenced under section 5 of this 2009 Act before January 2, 2012, shall continue to be governed by the provisions of section 5 of this 2009 Act.
(2) Nothing in the repeal of section 5 of this 2009 Act by section 14 of this 2009 Act or the amendments to ORS 166.250, 166.274, 166.291 and 166.470 by sections 10, 11, 11a and 20 of this 2009 Act affects the relief granted to a person under section 5 of this 2009 Act. [2009 c.826 §15; 2009 c.826 §24]

166.275 **Possession of weapons by inmates of institutions.** Any person committed to any institution who, while under the jurisdiction of any institution or while being conveyed to or from any institution, possesses or carries upon the person, or has under the custody or control of the person any dangerous instrument, or any weapon including but not limited to any blackjack, slingshot, billy, sand club, metal knuckles, explosive substance, dirk, dagger, sharp instrument, pistol, revolver or other firearm without lawful authority, is guilty of a felony and upon conviction thereof shall be punished by imprisonment in the custody of the Department of Corrections for a term not more than 20 years. [1953 c.533 §1; 1987 c.320 §88]

166.279 **Forfeiture of deadly weapons.** (1) Except as provided in subsection (4) of this section, ORS 131.550 to 131.600 do not apply to the forfeiture of a firearm or other deadly weapon that was possessed, used or available for use to facilitate a criminal offense.
(2) Except as provided in subsection (3) of this section, at the time of sentencing for any criminal offense in which a firearm or other deadly weapon was possessed, used or available for use to facilitate the offense, the court shall declare the weapon to be contraband and order that the weapon be forfeited.

(3) If a firearm or other deadly weapon that was possessed, used or available for use to facilitate a criminal offense was stolen from its lawful owner and was recovered from a person other than the lawful owner, the court may not order that the weapon be forfeited but shall order that the weapon be restored to the lawful owner as soon as the weapon is no longer needed for evidentiary purposes.

(4) The court shall release a firearm or other deadly weapon forfeited under subsection (2) of this section to the law enforcement agency that seized the weapon. The law enforcement agency may destroy or sell the weapon, use the weapon as a service weapon or use the weapon for training, identification or demonstration purposes. When a weapon is sold pursuant to this subsection, the law enforcement agency shall pay the proceeds from the sale, less the costs of the sale, as provided in ORS 131.594 and 131.597.

(5) As used in this section, "deadly weapon" has the meaning given that term in ORS 161.015. [2003 c.614 §4; 2005 c.830 §24]

166.280 [Amended by 1981 c.767 §1; 1993 c.625 §2; 1997 c.480 §5; 1997 c.693 §2; repealed by 2001 c.666 §56]

166.281 [2001 c.666 §52; repealed by 2003 c.614 §13]

166.282 Sale of weapons by political subdivision; disposition of proceeds. (1) A political subdivision in this state that sells a weapon described in subsection (2) of this section shall pay the proceeds from the sale of the weapon, less the costs of the sale, to the account of the police agency that received the weapon, to be used for purposes of public safety, law enforcement and crime prevention and detection.

(2) Subsection (1) of this section applies to a weapon that is donated to the police agency. [1997 c.693 §1; 2001 c.666 §§25,37; 2003 c.614 §5]

166.290 [Amended by 1973 c.391 §1; repealed by 1989 c.839 §7 (166.291 to 166.293 enacted in lieu of 166.290)]

166.291 Issuance of concealed handgun license; application; fees; liability. (1) The sheriff of a county, upon a person's application for an Oregon concealed handgun license, upon receipt of the appropriate fees and after compliance with the procedures set out in this section, shall issue the person a concealed

handgun license if the person:
(a)(A) Is a citizen of the United States; or
    (B) Is a legal resident alien who can document contin-
uous residency in the county for at least six months
and has declared in writing to the United States
Citizenship and Immigration Services the intent to
acquire citizenship status and can present proof of
the written declaration to the sheriff at the time of
application for the license;
(b) Is at least 21 years of age;
(c) Is a resident of the county;
(d) Has no outstanding warrants for arrest;
(e) Is not free on any form of pretrial release;
(f) Demonstrates competence with a handgun by any one
of the following:
    (A) Completion of any hunter education or hunter
safety course approved by the State Department of
Fish and Wildlife or a similar agency of another state if
handgun safety was a component of the course;
    (B) Completion of any National Rifle Association
firearms safety or training course if handgun safety
was a component of the course;
    (C) Completion of any firearms safety or training
course or class available to the general public offered
by law enforcement, community college, or private or
public institution or organization or firearms training
school utilizing instructors certified by the National
Rifle Association or a law enforcement agency if
handgun safety was a component of the course;
    (D) Completion of any law enforcement firearms safety
or training course or class offered for security guards,
investigators, reserve law enforcement officers or
any other law enforcement officers if handgun
safety was a component of the course;
    (E) Presents evidence of equivalent experience with a
handgun through participation in organized shooting
competition or military service;
    (F) Is licensed or has been licensed to carry a firearm
in this state, unless the license has been revoked; or
    (G) Completion of any firearms training or safety
course or class conducted by a firearms instructor
certified by a law enforcement agency or the National
Rifle Association if handgun safety was a component
of the course;

(g) Has never been convicted of a felony or found guilty, except for insanity under ORS 161.295, of a felony;

(h) Has not been convicted of a misdemeanor or found guilty, except for insanity under ORS 161.295, of a misdemeanor within the four years prior to the application;

(i) Has not been committed to the Oregon Health Authority under ORS 426.130;

(j) Has not been found to be mentally ill and is not subject to an order under ORS 426.130 that the person be prohibited from purchasing or possessing a firearm as a result of that mental illness;

(k) Has been discharged from the jurisdiction of the juvenile court for more than four years if, while a minor, the person was found to be within the jurisdiction of the juvenile court for having committed an act that, if committed by an adult, would constitute a felony or a misdemeanor involving violence, as defined in ORS 166.470;

(L) Has not been convicted of an offense involving controlled substances or participated in a court-supervised drug diversion program, except this disability does not operate to exclude a person if:

(A) The person has been convicted only once of violating ORS 475.864 (3) and has not completed a court-supervised drug diversion program under ORS 135.907; or

(B) The person has completed a court-supervised drug diversion program under ORS 135.907 and has not been convicted of violating ORS 475.864 (3);

(m) Is not subject to a citation issued under ORS 163.735 or an order issued under ORS 30.866, 107.700 to 107.735 or 163.738;

(n) Has not received a dishonorable discharge from the Armed Forces of the United States; and

(o) Is not required to register as a sex offender in any state.

(2) A person who has been granted relief under ORS 166.274 or 166.293 or 18 U.S.C. 925(c) or has had the person's record expunged under the laws of this state or equivalent laws of other jurisdictions is not subject to the disabilities in subsection (1)(g) to (L) of this section.

(3) Before the sheriff may issue a license:

(a) The application must state the applicant's legal name, current address and telephone number, date and place of birth, hair and eye color and height and weight. The application must also list the applicant's residence address or address-es for the previous three years. The application must contain a statement by the applicant that the applicant meets the requirements of subsection (1) of this section. The applica-tion may include the Social Security number of the applicant if the applicant voluntarily provides this number. The applica-tion must be signed by the applicant.

(b) The applicant must submit to fingerprinting and photo-graphing by the sheriff. The sheriff shall fingerprint and photograph the applicant and shall conduct any investiga-tion necessary to corroborate the requirements listed under subsection (1) of this section. If a nationwide crimi-nal records check is necessary, the sheriff shall request the Department of State Police to conduct the check, including fingerprint identification, through the Federal Bureau of Investigation. The Federal Bureau of Investigation shall return the fingerprint cards used to conduct the criminal records check and may not keep any record of the fingerprints. The Department of State Police shall report the results of the fingerprint-based criminal records check to the sheriff. The Department of State Police shall also furnish the sheriff with any information about the applicant that the Department of State Police may have in its possession from its central bureau of crim-inal identification including, but not limited to, manual or computerized criminal offender information.

(4) Application forms for concealed handgun licenses shall be supplied by the sheriff upon request. The forms shall be uni-form throughout the state in substantially the following form:

APPLICATION FOR LICENSE TO CARRY CONCEALED HANDGUN

Date_____

I hereby declare as follows:

I am a citizen of the United States or a legal resident alien who can document continuous residency in the county for at least six months and have declared in writing to the United States Citizenship and Immigration Services my intention to become a citizen and can present proof of the written declaration to the sheriff at the time of this application. I am at least 21 years of age. I have been discharged from the jurisdiction of the juvenile court for more than four years if, while a minor, I was found to be within the jurisdiction of the juvenile court for having committed an act that, if committed by an adult, would constitute a felony or a misdemeanor involving violence, as defined in ORS 166.470. I have never been convicted of a felony or found guilty, except for insanity under ORS 161.295, of a felony in the State of Oregon or elsewhere. I have not, within the last four years, been convicted of a misdemeanor or found guilty, except for insanity under ORS 161.295, of a misdemeanor. Except as provided in ORS 166.291 (1)(L), I have not been convicted of an offense involving controlled substances or completed a court-supervised drug diversion program. There are no outstanding warrants for my arrest and I am not free on any form of pretrial release. I have not been committed to the Oregon Health Authority under ORS 426.130, nor have I been found mentally ill and presently subject to an order prohibiting me from purchasing or possessing a firearm because of mental illness. If any of the previous conditions do apply to me, I have been granted relief or wish to petition for relief from the disability under ORS 166.274 or 166.293 or 18 U.S.C. 925(c) or have had the records expunged. I am not subject to a citation issued under ORS 163.735 or an order issued under ORS 30.866, 107.700 to 107.735 or 163.738. I have never received a dishonorable discharge from the Armed Forces of the United States. I am not required to register as a sex offender in any state. I understand I will be fingerprinted and photographed.

Legal name _____

Age _____ Date of birth _____

Place of birth _____

Social Security number _____

(Disclosure of your Social Security account number is voluntary. Solicitation of the number is authorized under ORS 166.291. It will be used only as a means of identification.)

Proof of identification (Two pieces of current identification are required, one of which must bear a photograph of the applicant. The type of identification and the number on the identification are to be filled in by the sheriff.):

1. _____

2. _____

Height _____ Weight _____
Hair color _____ Eye color _____

Current address _____
(List residence addresses for the past three years on the back.)
City _____ County _____ Zip _____
Phone _____

I have read the entire text of this application, and the statements therein are correct and true. (Making false statements on this application is a misdemeanor.)

_____

(Signature of Applicant)

Character references.

_____

   Name   Address

_____

   Name   Address
Approved ___ Disapproved ___ by ___

Competence with handgun demonstrated by _____
(to be filled in by sheriff)
Date _____ Fee Paid _____
License No._____

---

(5)(a) Fees for concealed handgun licenses are:
    (A) $15 to the Department of State Police for conducing the fingerprint check of the applicant.
    (B) $50 to the sheriff for the issuance or renewal of a concealed handgun license.
    (C) $15 to the sheriff for the duplication of a license because of loss or change of address.
  (b) The sheriff may enter into an agreement with the Department of Transportation to produce the concealed handgun license.
(6) No civil or criminal liability shall attach to the sheriff or any authorized representative engaged in the receipt and review of, or an investigation connected with, any application for, or in the issuance, denial or revocation of, any license under ORS

166.291 to 166.295 as a result of the lawful performance of duties under those sections.

(7) Immediately upon acceptance of an application for a concealed handgun license, the sheriff shall enter the applicant's name into the Law Enforcement Data System indicating that the person is an applicant for a concealed handgun license or is a license holder.

(8) The county sheriff may waive the residency requirement in subsection (1)(c) of this section for a resident of a contiguous state who has a compelling business interest or other legitimate demonstrated need.

(9) For purposes of subsection (1)(c) of this section, a person is a resident of a county if the person:

(a) Has a current Oregon driver license issued to the person showing a residence address in the county;

(b) Is registered to vote in the county and has a memorandum card issued to the person under ORS 247.181 showing a residence address in the county;

(c) Has documentation showing that the person currently leases or owns real property in the county; or

(d) Has documentation showing that the person filed an Oregon tax return for the most recent tax year showing a residence address in the county.

166.292 Procedure for issuing; form of license; duration. (1) If the application for the license is approved, the sheriff shall issue and mail or otherwise deliver to the applicant at the address shown on the application, within 45 days of the application, a wallet sized license bearing the photograph of the licensee. The license must be signed by the licensee and carried whenever the licensee carries a concealed handgun.

(2) Failure of a person who carries a concealed handgun also to carry a concealed handgun license is prima facie evidence that the person does not have such a license.

(3) Licenses for concealed handguns shall be uniform throughout the state in substantially the following form:

OREGON CONCEALED HANDGUN LICENSE

County _____ License Number_____

Expires_____ Date of birth _____

Height _____ Weight_____
Name _____ Address _____
Licensee's City_____ Zip_____ Photograph _____
Signature _____
Issued by _____
Date of issue _____

---

(4) An Oregon concealed handgun license issued under ORS 166.291 and this section, unless revoked under ORS 166.293, is valid for a period of four years from the date on which it is issued.
(5) The sheriff shall keep a record of each license issued under ORS 166.291 and this section, or renewed pursuant to ORS 166.295.
(6) When a sheriff issues a concealed handgun license under this section, the sheriff shall provide the licensee with a list of those places where carrying concealed handguns is prohibited or restricted by state or federal law. [1989 c.839 §9 (166.291 to 166.293 enacted in lieu of 166.290); 1993 c.625 §5; 1993 c.693 §2; 1993 c.735 §5]

166.293 Denial or revocation of license; review. (1) If the application for the concealed handgun license is denied, the sheriff shall set forth in writing the reasons for the denial. The denial shall be sent to the applicant by certified mail, restricted delivery, within 45 days after the application was made. If no decision is issued within 45 days, the person may seek review under the procedures in subsection (5) of this section.
(2) Notwithstanding ORS 166.291 (1), and subject to review as provided in subsection (5) of this section, a sheriff may deny a concealed handgun license if the sheriff has reasonable grounds to believe that the applicant has been or is reasonably likely to be a danger to self or others, or to the community at large, as a result of the applicant's mental or psychological state or as demonstrated by the applicant's past pattern of behavior involving unlawful violence or threats of unlawful violence.
(3)(a) Any act or condition that would prevent the issuance of a concealed handgun license is cause for revoking a concealed handgun license.
   (b) A sheriff may revoke a concealed handgun license by serving upon the licensee a notice of revocation. The notice must contain the grounds for the revocation and

must be served either personally or by certified mail, restricted delivery. The notice and return of service shall be included in the file of the licensee. The revocation is effective upon the licensee's receipt of the notice.

(4) Any peace officer or corrections officer may seize a concealed handgun license and return it to the issuing sheriff if the license is held by a person who has been arrested or cited for a crime that can or would otherwise disqualify the person from being issued a concealed handgun license. The issuing sheriff shall hold the license for 30 days. If the person is not charged with a crime within the 30 days, the sheriff shall return the license unless the sheriff revokes the license as provided in subsection (3) of this section.

(5) A person denied a concealed handgun license or whose license is revoked or not renewed under ORS 166.291 to 166.295 may petition the circuit court in the petitioner's county of residence to review the denial, nonrenewal or revocation. The petition must be filed within 30 days after the receipt of the notice of denial or revocation.

(6) The judgment affirming or overturning the sheriff's decision shall be based on whether the petitioner meets the criteria that are used for issuance of a concealed handgun license and, if the petitioner was denied a concealed handgun license, whether the sheriff has reasonable grounds for denial under subsection (2) of this section. Whenever the petitioner has been previously sentenced for a crime under ORS 161.610 or for a crime of violence for which the person could have received a sentence of more than 10 years, the court shall grant relief only if the court finds that relief should be granted in the interest of justice.

(7) Notwithstanding the provisions of ORS 9.320, a corporation, the state or any city, county, district or other political subdivision or public corporation in this state, without appearance by attorney, may appear as a party to an action under this section.

(8) Petitions filed under this section shall be heard and disposed of within 15 judicial days of filing or as soon as practicable thereafter.

(9) Filing fees for actions shall be as for any civil action filed in the court. If the petitioner prevails, the amount of the filing fee shall be paid by the respondent to the petitioner and may be incorporated into the court order.

(10) Initial appeals of petitions shall be heard de novo.

(11) Any party to a judgment under this section may appeal to

the Court of Appeals in the same manner as for any other civil action.

(12) If the governmental entity files an appeal under this section and does not prevail, it shall be ordered to pay the attorney fees for the prevailing party. [1989 c.839 §9a (166.291 to 166.293 enacted in lieu of 166.290); 1993 c.735 §6; 1995 c.518 §3; 1995 c.658 §89; 1999 c.1052 §7; 2003 c.14 §65; 2007 c.202 §1; 2007 c.368 §3]

166.295 Renewal of license. (1)(a) A concealed handgun license is renewable by repeating the procedures set out in ORS 166.291 and 166.292, except for the requirement to submit fingerprints and provide character references. A licensee may submit the application for renewal by mail if the licensee:

(A) Is an active member of the Armed Forces of the United States, the National Guard of the United States or the Oregon National Guard; and

(B) Submits with the application proof of the licensee's military orders and a copy of the licensee's military identification.

(b) An otherwise expired concealed handgun license continues to be valid for up to 45 days after the licensee applies for renewal if:

(A) The licensee applies for renewal before the original license expires;

(B) The licensee has proof of the application for renewal; and

(C) The application for renewal has not been denied.

(2) If a licensee changes residence, the licensee shall report the change of address and the sheriff shall issue a new license as a duplication for a change of address. The license shall expire upon the same date as would the original. [1989 c.839 §10; 1993 c.735 §7; 2007 c.368 §4]

166.297 Annual report regarding revocation of licenses. (1) The sheriff of a county shall submit annually to the Department of State Police a report containing the number of concealed handgun licenses revoked during the reporting period and the reasons for the revocations.

(2) The Department of State Police shall compile the reports submitted under subsection (1) of this section and shall submit the compilation to the Legislative Assembly biennially. [1993 c.735 §13]

166.300 Killing another as cause for loss of right to bear arms. (1) Any person who has committed, with firearms of any kind or description, murder in any degree, or manslaughter, either voluntary or involuntary, or who in a careless or reckless manner, kills or injures another with firearms, and who, at any time after committing murder or manslaughter or after said careless or reckless killing or injury of another, carries or bears firearms of any kind or description within this state, shall be punished upon conviction by a fine of not more than $500, or by imprisonment in the county jail not to exceed one year, or both.

(2) Subsection (1) of this section does not deprive the people of this state of the right to bear arms for the defense of themselves and the state, and does not apply to any peace officer in the discharge of official duties or to a member of any regularly constituted military organization while on duty with such military organization.

(3) Justice courts, county courts and all other courts having jurisdiction as justice courts, shall have concurrent jurisdiction with the circuit courts of all prosecutions under subsection (1) of this section.

166.310 [Repealed by 1985 c.709 §4]

166.320 Setting springgun or setgun. (1) Any person who places or sets any loaded springgun, setgun, or any gun, firearm or other device of any kind designed for containing or firing explosives, in any place where it may be fired, exploded or discharged by the contact of any person or animal with any string, wire, rod, stick, spring or other contrivance affixed to or connected with it, or with its trigger, shall be punished upon conviction by a fine of not less than $100 nor more than $500, or by imprisonment in the county jail for not less than 30 days nor more than six months, or both.

(2) Subsection (1) of this section does not apply to any loaded springgun, setgun, firearm or other device placed for the purpose of destroying gophers, moles or other burrowing rodents, and does not prevent the use of a coyote getter by employees of county, state or federal governments engaged in cooperative predatory animal control work.

166.330 Use of firearms with other than incombustible gun wadding. Any person who uses in any firearms discharged on lands within this state, not owned by the person, anything other than incombustible gun wadding, shall be punished upon conviction by a fine of not less than $5 nor more than $100, or by imprisonment in the county jail for not less than two days nor more than 60 days.

166.340 [1965 c.20 §§2,3; 1969 c.351 §1; repealed by 1981 c.41 §3]

166.350 Unlawful possession of armor piercing ammunition. (1) A person commits the crime of unlawful possession of armor piercing ammunition if the person:

(a) Makes, sells, buys or possesses any handgun ammunition the bullet or projectile of which is coated with Teflon or any chemical compound with properties similar to Teflon and which is intended to penetrate soft body armor, such person having the intent that the ammunition be used in the commission of a felony; or

(b) Carries any ammunition described in paragraph (a) of this subsection while committing any felony during which the person or any accomplice of the person is armed with a firearm.

(2) As used in this section, "handgun ammunition" means ammunition principally for use in pistols or revolvers notwithstanding that the ammunition can be used in some rifles.

(3) Unlawful possession of armor piercing ammunition is a Class A misdemeanor. [1985 c.755 §2; 1987 c.158 §29]

POSSESSION OF WEAPON OR DESTRUCTIVE DEVICE IN PUBLIC BUILDING OR COURT FACILITY

166.360 Definitions for ORS 166.360 to 166.380. As used in ORS 166.360 to 166.380, unless the context requires otherwise:

(1) "Capitol building" means the Capitol, the State Office Building, the State Library Building, the Labor and Industries Building, the State Transportation Building, the Agriculture Building or the Public Service Building and includes any new buildings which may be constructed on the same grounds as an addition to the group of buildings listed in this subsection.

(2) "Court facility" means a courthouse or that portion of any other building occupied by a circuit court, the Court of Appeals, the Supreme Court or the Oregon Tax Court or occupied by personnel related to the operations of those courts, or in which activities related to the operations of those courts take place.

(3) "Loaded firearm" means:

(a) A breech-loading firearm in which there is an unexpended cartridge or shell in or attached to the firearm including but not limited to, in a chamber, magazine or clip which is attached to the firearm.

(b) A muzzle-loading firearm which is capped or primed and has a powder charge and ball, shot or projectile in the barrel or cylinder.

(4) "Public building" means a hospital, a capitol building, a public or private school, as defined in ORS 339.315, a college or university, a city hall or the residence of any state official elected by the state at large, and the grounds adjacent to each such building. The term also includes that portion of any other building occupied by an agency of the state or a municipal corporation, as defined in ORS 297.405, other than a court facility.

(5) "Weapon" means:

(a) A firearm;

(b) Any dirk, dagger, ice pick, slingshot, metal knuckles or any similar instrument or a knife other than an ordinary pocket knife, the use of which could inflict injury upon a person or property;

(c) Mace, tear gas, pepper mace or any similar deleterious agent as defined in ORS 163.211;

(d) An electrical stun gun or any similar instrument;

(e) A tear gas weapon as defined in ORS 163.211;

(f) A club, bat, baton, billy club, bludgeon, knobkerrie, nunchaku, nightstick, truncheon or any similar instrument, the use of which could inflict injury upon a person or property; or

(g) A dangerous or deadly weapon as those terms are defined in ORS 161.015. [1969 c.705 §1; 1977 c.769 §2; 1979 c.398 §1; 1989 c.982 §4; 1993 c.741 §2; 1999 c.577 §2; 1999 c.782 §6; 2001 c.201 §1]

166.370 **Possession of firearm or dangerous weapon in public building or court facility; exceptions; discharging firearm at school.** (1) Any person who intentionally possesses a loaded or unloaded firearm or any other instrument used as a dangerous weapon, while in or on a public building, shall upon conviction be guilty of a Class C felony.

(2)(a) Except as otherwise provided in paragraph (b) of this subsection, a person who intentionally possesses:

(A) A firearm in a court facility is guilty, upon conviction, of a Class C felony. A person who intentionally possesses a firearm in a court facility shall surrender the firearm to a law enforcement officer.

(B) A weapon, other than a firearm, in a court facility may be required to surrender the weapon to a law enforcement officer or to immediately remove it from the court facility. A person who fails to comply with this subparagraph is guilty, upon conviction, of a Class C felony.

(b) The presiding judge of a judicial district may enter an order permitting the possession of specified weapons in a court facility.

(3) Subsection (1) of this section does not apply to:

(a) A sheriff, police officer, other duly appointed peace officers or a corrections officer while acting within the scope of employment.

(b) A person summoned by a peace officer to assist in making an arrest or preserving the peace, while the summoned person is engaged in assisting the officer.

(c) An active or reserve member of the military forces of this state or the United States, when engaged in the performance of duty.

(d) A person who is licensed under ORS 166.291 and 166.292 to carry a concealed handgun.

(e) A person who is authorized by the officer or agency that controls the public building to possess a firearm or dangerous weapon in that public building.

(f) An employee of the United States Department of Agriculture, acting within the scope of employment, who possesses a firearm in the course of the lawful taking of wildlife.

(g) Possession of a firearm on school property if the firearm:

(A) Is possessed by a person who is not otherwise prohibited from possessing the firearm; and

(B) Is unloaded and locked in a motor vehicle.

(4) The exceptions listed in subsection (3)(b) to (g) of this section constitute affirmative defenses to a charge of violating subsection (1) of this section.

(5)(a) Any person who knowingly, or with reckless disregard for the safety of another, discharges or attempts to discharge a firearm at a place that the person knows is a school shall upon conviction be guilty of a Class C felony.

(b) Paragraph (a) of this subsection does not apply to the discharge of a firearm:

(A) As part of a program approved by a school in the school by an individual who is participating in the program;

(B) By a law enforcement officer acting in the officer's official capacity; or

(C) By an employee of the United States Department of Agriculture, acting within the scope of employment, in the course of the lawful taking of wildlife.

(6) Any weapon carried in violation of this section is subject to the forfeiture provisions of ORS 166.279.

(7) Notwithstanding the fact that a person's conduct in a single criminal episode constitutes a violation of both subsections (1) and (5) of this section, the district attorney may charge the person with only one of the offenses.

(8) As used in this section, "dangerous weapon" means a dangerous weapon as that term is defined in ORS 161.015. [1969 c.705 §§2,4; 1977 c.207 §2; 1979 c.398 §2; 1989 c.839 §22; 1989 c.982 §5; 1991 c.67 §39; 1993 c.625 §1; 1999 c.782 §7; 1999 c.1040 §4; 2001 c.666 §§24,36; 2003 c.614 §6; 2009 c.556 §6]

166.372 [1993 c.625 §3; repealed by 1996 c.16 §5]

166.373 Possession of weapon in court facility by peace officer or federal officer. (1) Notwithstanding ORS 166.370 (2) and except as provided in subsection (2) of this section, a peace officer, as defined in ORS 161.015, or a federal officer, as defined in ORS 133.005, may possess a weapon in a court facility if the officer:

(a) Is acting in an official capacity and is officially on duty;

(b) Is carrying a weapon that the employing agency of the officer has authorized the officer to carry; and

(c) Is in compliance with any security procedures established under subsections (3) and (4) of this section.

(2) A judge may prohibit a peace officer or a federal officer from possessing a weapon in a courtroom. A notice of the prohibition of the possession of a weapon by an officer in a courtroom must be posted outside the entrance to the courtroom.

(3) A presiding judge of a judicial district or the Chief Justice of the Supreme Court may establish procedures regulating the possession of a weapon in a court facility by a peace officer or a federal officer subject to the following:

(a) The procedures must be established through a plan for court security improvement, emergency preparedness and business continuity under ORS 1.177 or 1.180; and

(b) Notice of the procedures must be posted at the entrance to the court facility, or at an entrance for peace officers or federal officers if the entrance is separate from the entrance to the court facility, and at a security checkpoint in the court facility.

(4) A judge may establish procedures regulating the possession of a weapon in a courtroom by a peace officer or a federal officer. A notice of the procedures regulating the possession of a weapon by an officer must be posted outside the entrance to the courtroom. [2001 c.201 §3; 2005 c.804 §7]

166.380 Examination of firearm by peace officer; arrest for failure to allow examination. (1) A peace officer may examine a firearm possessed by anyone on the person while in or on a public building to determine whether the firearm is a loaded firearm.

(2) Refusal by a person to allow the examination authorized by subsection (1) of this section constitutes reason to believe that the person has committed a crime and the peace officer may make an arrest pursuant to ORS 133.310. [1969 c.705 §3]

166.382 Possession of destructive device prohibited; exceptions. (1) A person commits the crime of unlawful possession of a destructive device if the person possesses:

(a) Any of the following devices with an explosive, incendiary or poison gas component:

(A) Bomb;

(B) Grenade;

(C) Rocket having a propellant charge of more than four ounces;

(D) Missile having an explosive or incendiary charge of more than one-quarter ounce; or

(E) Mine; or

(b) Any combination of parts either designed or intended for use in converting any device into any destructive device described in paragraph (a) of this subsection and from which a destructive device may be readily assembled.

(2) As used in this section:

(a) "Destructive device" does not include any device which is designed primarily or redesigned primarily for use as a signaling, pyrotechnic, line throwing, safety or similar device.

(b) "Possess" has the meaning given that term in ORS 161.015.

(3) This section does not apply to:

(a) Persons who possess explosives as provided in ORS 480.200 to 480.290.

(b) The possession of an explosive by a member of the Armed Forces of the United States while on active duty and engaged in the performance of official duties or by a member of a regularly organized fire or police department of a public agency while engaged in the performance of official duties.

(c) The possession of an explosive in the course of transportation by way of railroad, water, highway or air while under the jurisdiction of, or in conformity with, regulations adopted by the United States Department of Transportation.

(d) The possession, sale, transfer or manufacture of an explosive by a person acting in accordance with the provisions of any applicable federal law or regulation that provides substantially the same requirements as the comparable provisions of ORS 480.200 to 480.290.

(4) Possession of a destructive device is a Class C felony. [1989 c.982 §1]

166.384 Unlawful manufacture of destructive device. (1) A person commits the crime of unlawful manufacture of a destructive device if the person assembles, produces or otherwise manufactures:

(a) A destructive device, as defined in ORS 166.382; or

(b) A pyrotechnic device containing two or more grains of pyrotechnic charge in violation of chapter 10, Title 18 of the United States Code.

(2) Unlawful manufacture of a destructive device is a Class C felony. [1989 c.982 §2]

166.385 Possession of hoax destructive device. (1) A person commits the crime of possession of a hoax destructive device if the person knowingly places another person in fear of serious physical injury by:

(a) Possessing, manufacturing, selling, delivering, placing or causing to be placed a hoax destructive device; or

(b) Sending a hoax destructive device to another person.

(2) Possession of a hoax destructive device is a Class A misdemeanor.

(3) Notwithstanding subsection (2) of this section, possession of a hoax destructive device is a Class C felony if a person possesses, or threatens to use, a hoax destructive device while

the person is committing or attempting to commit a felony.
(4) As used in this section, "hoax destructive device" means an object that reasonably appears, under the circumstances:
(a) To be a destructive device, as described in ORS 166.382 (1)(a), or an explosive, as defined in ORS 166.660, but is an inoperative imitation of a destructive device or explosive; or
    (b) To contain a destructive device, as described in ORS 166.382 (1)(a), or an explosive, as defined in ORS 166.660. [1997 c.749 §1]

SALE OR TRANSFER OF FIREARMS

166.410 Manufacture, importation or sale of firearms. Any person who manufactures or causes to be manufactured within this state, or who imports into this state, or offers, exposes for sale, or sells or transfers a handgun, short-barreled rifle, short-barreled shotgun, firearms silencer or machine gun, otherwise than in accordance with ORS 166.250, 166.260, 166.270, 166.291, 166.292, 166.425, 166.450, 166.460 and 166.470, is guilty of a Class B felony. [Amended by 1979 c.779 §5; 1987 c.320 §89; 1989 c.839 §23; 1995 c.729 §7; 2001 c.666 §§34,46; 2003 c.14 §§66,67; 2003 c.614 §9]

166.412 Definitions; firearms transaction record; criminal record check; rules. (1) As used in this section:
    (a) "Antique firearm" has the meaning given that term in 18 U.S.C. 921;
    (b) "Department" means the Department of State Police;
    (c) "Firearm" has the meaning given that term in ORS 166.210, except that it does not include an antique firearm;
    (d) "Firearms transaction record" means the firearms transaction record required by 18 U.S.C. 921 to 929;
    (e) "Firearms transaction thumbprint form" means a form provided by the department under subsection (11) of this section;
    (f) "Gun dealer" means a person engaged in the business, as defined in 18 U.S.C. 921, of selling, leasing or otherwise transferring a firearm, whether the person is a retail dealer, pawnbroker or otherwise;
    (g) "Handgun" has the meaning given that term in ORS 166.210; and
    (h) "Purchaser" means a person who buys, leases or otherwise receives a firearm from a gun dealer.

(2) Except as provided in subsections (3)(c) and (12) of this section, a gun dealer shall comply with the following before a handgun is delivered to a purchaser:

(a) The purchaser shall present to the dealer current identification meeting the requirements of subsection (4) of this section.

(b) The gun dealer shall complete the firearms transaction record and obtain the signature of the purchaser on the record.

(c) The gun dealer shall obtain the thumbprints of the purchaser on the firearms transaction thumbprint form and attach the form to the gun dealer's copy of the firearms transaction record to be filed with that copy.

(d) The gun dealer shall request by telephone that the department conduct a criminal history record check on the purchaser and shall provide the following information to the department:

(A) The federal firearms license number of the gun dealer;

(B) The business name of the gun dealer;

(C) The place of transfer;

(D) The name of the person making the transfer;

(E) The make, model, caliber and manufacturer's number of the handgun being transferred;

(F) The name and date of birth of the purchaser;

(G) The Social Security number of the purchaser if the purchaser voluntarily provides this number to the gun dealer; and

(H) The type, issuer and identification number of the identification presented by the purchaser.

(e) The gun dealer shall receive a unique approval number for the transfer from the department and record the approval number on the firearms transaction record and on the firearms transaction thumbprint form.

(f) The gun dealer may destroy the firearms transaction thumbprint form five years after the completion of the firearms transaction thumbprint form.

(3)(a) Upon receipt of a request of the gun dealer for a criminal history record check, the department shall immediately, during the gun dealer's telephone call or by return call:

(A) Determine, from criminal records and other information available to it, whether the purchaser is disqualified under ORS 166.470 from completing the purchase; and

(B) Notify the dealer when a purchaser is disqualified from completing the transfer or provide the dealer with a unique approval number indicating that the purchaser is qualified to complete the transfer.

(b) If the department is unable to determine if the purchaser is qualified or disqualified from completing the transfer within 30 minutes, the department shall notify the dealer and provide the dealer with an estimate of the time when the department will provide the requested information.

(c) If the department fails to provide a unique approval number to a gun dealer or to notify the gun dealer that the purchaser is disqualified under paragraph (a) of this subsection before the close of the gun dealer's next business day following the request by the dealer for a criminal history record check, the dealer may deliver the handgun to the purchaser.

(4)(a) Identification required of the purchaser under subsection (2) of this section shall include one piece of current identification bearing a photograph and the date of birth of the purchaser that:

(A) Is issued under the authority of the United States Government, a state, a political subdivision of a state, a foreign government, a political subdivision of a foreign government, an international governmental organization or an international quasi-governmental organization; and

(B) Is intended to be used for identification of an individual or is commonly accepted for the purpose of identification of an individual.

(b) If the identification presented by the purchaser under paragraph (a) of this subsection does not include the current address of the purchaser, the purchaser shall present a second piece of current identification that contains the current address of the purchaser. The Superintendent of State Police may specify by rule the type of identification that may be presented under this paragraph.

(c) The department may require that the dealer verify the identification of the purchaser if that identity is in question by sending the thumbprints of the purchaser to the department.

(5) The department shall establish a telephone number that shall be operational seven days a week between the hours of 8 a.m. and 10 p.m. for the purpose of responding to inquiries from dealers for a criminal history record check under this section.

(6) No public employee, official or agency shall be held criminally or civilly liable for performing the investigations required by this section provided the employee, official or agency acts in good faith and without malice.

(7)(a) The department may retain a record of the information obtained during a request for a criminal records check for no more than five years.

(b) The record of the information obtained during a request for a criminal records check by a gun dealer is exempt from disclosure under public records law.

(8) A law enforcement agency may inspect the records of a gun dealer relating to transfers of handguns with the consent of a gun dealer in the course of a reasonable inquiry during a criminal investigation or under the authority of a properly authorized subpoena or search warrant.

(9) When a handgun is delivered, it shall be unloaded.

(10) In accordance with applicable provisions of ORS chapter 183, the Superintendent of State Police may adopt rules necessary for:

(a) The design of the firearms transaction thumbprint form;

(b) The maintenance of a procedure to correct errors in the criminal records of the department;

(c) The provision of a security system to identify dealers who request a criminal history record check under subsection (2) of this section; and

(d) The creation and maintenance of a database of the business hours of gun dealers.

(11) The department shall publish the firearms transaction thumbprint form and shall furnish the form to gun dealers on application at cost.

(12) This section does not apply to transactions between persons licensed as dealers under 18 U.S.C. 923. [1995 c.729 §1; 2001 c.900 §25; 2009 c.595 §114; 2009 c.826 §17]

Note: Section 12 (2)(b) and (3)(b), chapter 826, Oregon Laws 2009, affects the implementation of amendments to 166.412 by section 17, chapter 826, Oregon Laws 2009. Section 12, chapter 826, Oregon Laws 2009, provides:

Sec. 12. (1) Section 1 of this 2009 Act [181.740] applies to records and information in the possession of the Department of Human Services, the Oregon Health Authority, the Psychiatric Security Review Board or the Judicial Department on or after the effective date of this 2009 Act [January 1, 2010], irrespective of when the record or information was created.

(2)(a) When the Department of Human Services determines that the department has received a sufficient legislative appropriation or federal funding to carry out the provisions of section 1 of this 2009 Act, the department shall adopt a rule so indicating. The department shall notify Legislative Counsel when the rule is adopted.

(b) When the Oregon Health Authority determines that the authority has received a sufficient legislative appropriation or federal funding to carry out the provisions of section 1 of this 2009 Act, the authority shall adopt a rule so indicating. The authority shall notify Legislative Counsel when the rule is adopted.

(c) When the Chief Justice of the Supreme Court determines that the Judicial Department has received a sufficient legislative appropriation or federal funding to carry out the provisions of section 1 of this 2009 Act, the Chief Justice shall issue an order so indicating. The Chief Justice shall notify Legislative Counsel when the order is issued.

(d) When the Psychiatric Security Review Board determines that the board has received a sufficient legislative appropriation or federal funding to carry out the provisions of section 1 of this 2009 Act, the board shall adopt a rule so indicating. The board shall notify Legislative Counsel when the rule is adopted.

(3)(a)(A) The Department of Human Services may not comply with section 1 of this 2009 Act until the department adopts the rule described in subsection (2)(a) of this section; and

(B) If the Department of Human Services adopts the rule described in subsection (2)(a) of this section before January 2, 2012, the department may not comply with section 1 of this 2009 Act until the later of:

(i) The date the Psychiatric Security Review Board adopts the rule described in section 13 of this 2009 Act; or

(ii) January 2, 2012.

(b)(A) The Oregon Health Authority may not comply with section 1 of this 2009 Act or the amendments to ORS 166.412 by section 17 of this 2009 Act until the authority adopts the rule described in subsection (2)(b) of this section; and

(B) If the Oregon Health Authority adopts the rule described in subsection (2)(b) of this section before

January 2, 2012, the authority may not comply with section 1 of this 2009 Act or the amendments to ORS 166.412 by section 17 of this 2009 Act until the later of:
    (i) The date the Psychiatric Security Review Board adopts the rule described in section 13 of this 2009 Act; or
    (ii) January 2, 2012.

(c)(A) The Judicial Department may not comply with section 1 of this 2009 Act until the Chief Justice issues the order described in subsection (2)(c) of this section; and
    (B) If the Chief Justice issues the order described in subsection (2)(c) of this section before January 2, 2012, the Judicial Department may not comply with section 1 of this 2009 Act until the later of:
    (i) The date the Psychiatric Security Review Board adopts the rule described in section 13 of this 2009 Act; or
    (ii) January 2, 2012.

(d)(A) The Psychiatric Security Review Board may not comply with section 1 of this 2009 Act until the board adopts the rule described in subsection (2)(d) of this section; and
    (B) If the board adopts the rule described in subsection (2)(d) of this section before January 2, 2012, the board may not comply with section 1 of this 2009 Act until the later of:
    (i) The date the board adopts the rule described in section 13 of this 2009 Act; or
    (ii) January 2, 2012.

(4)(a) When the Chief Justice of the Supreme Court determines that the Judicial Department has received a sufficient legislative appropriation or federal funding to carry out the provisions of the amendments to ORS 426.160 and 427.293 by sections 2 and 3 of this 2009 Act, the Chief Justice shall issue an order so indicating. The Chief Justice shall notify Legislative Counsel when the order is issued.
    (b)(A) Except as provided in subparagraph (B) of this paragraph, the amendments to ORS 426.160 and 427.293 by sections 2 and 3 of this 2009 Act become operative on the date the Chief Justice issues the order described in paragraph (a) of this subsection.
    (B) If the Chief Justice issues the order described in paragraph (a) of this subsection before January 2, 2012, the amendments to ORS 426.160 and 427.293

by sections 2 and 3 of this 2009 Act become operative on the later of:
(i) The date the Psychiatric Security Review Board adopts the rule described in section 13 of this 2009 Act; or
(ii) January 2, 2012. [2009 c.826 §12; 2009 c.826 §21]

Note: 166.412 to 166.421 were enacted into law by the Legislative Assembly but were not added to or made a part of ORS chapter 166 or any series therein by legislative action. See Preface to Oregon Revised Statutes for further explanation.

166.414 Fees for conducting criminal history record checks. (1) The Department of State Police may adopt a fee schedule for criminal history record checks required under ORS 166.412 and collect a fee for each criminal history record check requested. The fee schedule shall be calculated to recover the cost of performing criminal history record checks required under ORS 166.412, but may not exceed $10 per record check.
(2) Fees collected under this section shall be paid into the State Treasury and deposited in the General Fund to the credit of the State Police Account. [1995 c.729 §2]

Note: See second note under 166.412.

166.416 Providing false information in connection with a transfer of a firearm. (1) A person commits the crime of providing false information in connection with a transfer of a firearm if the person knowingly provides a false name or false information or presents false identification in connection with a purchase or transfer of a firearm.
(2) Providing false information in connection with a transfer of a firearm is a Class A misdemeanor. [1995 c.729 §3; 2001 c.1 §9]

Note: See second note under 166.412.

166.418 Improperly transferring a firearm. (1) A person commits the crime of improperly transferring a firearm if the person is a gun dealer as defined in ORS 166.412 and sells, leases or otherwise transfers a firearm and intentionally violates ORS 166.412 or 166.434.

(2) Improperly transferring a firearm is a Class A misdemeanor. [1995 c.729 §4; 2001 c.1 §10]

Note: See second note under 166.412.

166.420 [Amended by 1989 c.839 §2; 1993 c.4 §1; 1993 c.594 §4; 1993 c.693 §1; repealed by 1995 c.729 §13]

166.421 Stolen firearms; determination; telephone requests. The Department of State Police may respond to a telephone request from any person requesting that the department determine if department records show that a firearm is stolen. No public employee, official or agency shall be held criminally or civilly liable for performing the investigation allowed by this section provided that the employee, official or agency acts in good faith and without malice. [1995 c.729 §5]

Note: See second note under 166.412.

166.422 Enforcement of ORS 166.412. Where appropriate, a person may enforce the legal duties imposed by ORS 166.412 (7), by the provisions of ORS 30.260 to 30.300 and ORS chapter 183. [1989 c.839 §12; 1995 c.729 §8]

Note: 166.422 was enacted into law by the Legislative Assembly but was not added to or made a part of ORS chapter 166 or any series therein by legislative action. See Preface to Oregon Revised Statutes for further explanation.

166.425 Unlawful purchase of firearm. (1) A person commits the crime of unlawfully purchasing a firearm if the person, knowing that the person is prohibited by state or federal law from owning or possessing the firearm or having the firearm under the person's custody or control, purchases or attempts to purchase the firearm.

(2) Unlawfully purchasing a firearm is a Class A misdemeanor. [1989 c.839 §15]

166.427 Register of transfers of used firearms. (1) Whenever a person engaged in the business, as defined in 18 U.S.C. 921, of selling, leasing or otherwise transferring a firearm, whether the person is a retail dealer, pawnbroker or otherwise, buys or accepts in trade, a used firearm, the person shall enter in a register the time, date and place of purchase or trade, the name of the person selling or trading the firearm, the number of the identification documentation presented by the person and the make, model and manufacturer's number of the firearm. The register shall be obtained from and furnished by the Department of State Police to the dealer on application at cost.

(2) The duplicate sheet of the register shall, on the day of purchase or trade, be hand delivered or mailed to the local law enforcement authority.

(3) Violation of this section by any person engaged in the business of selling, leasing or otherwise transferring a firearm is a Class C misdemeanor. [1989 c.839 §16; 1993 c.4 §3; 2001 c.539 §12]

166.429 Firearms used in felony. Any person who, with intent to commit a felony or who knows or reasonably should know that a felony will be committed with the firearm, ships, transports, receives, sells or otherwise furnishes any firearm in the furtherance of the felony is guilty of a Class B felony. [1989 c.839 §17]

166.430 [Amended by 1971 c.464 §1; repealed by 1989 c.839 §39]

166.432 Definitions for ORS 166.412 and 166.433 to 166.441. (1) As used in ORS 166.412, 166.433, 166.434, 166.436 and 166.438, "criminal background check" or "criminal history record check" means determining the eligibility of a person to purchase or possess a firearm by reviewing state and federal databases including, but not limited to, the:

(a) Oregon computerized criminal history system;

(b) Oregon mental health data system;

(c) Law Enforcement Data System;

(d) National Instant Criminal Background Check System; and

(e) Stolen guns system.

(2) As used in ORS 166.433, 166.434, 166.436, 166.438 and 166.441:

(a) "Gun dealer" has the meaning given that term in ORS 166.412.

(b) "Gun show" means an event at which more than 25 firearms are on site and available for transfer. [2001 c.1 §3]

Note: 166.432, 166.433 and 166.445 were adopted by the people by initiative petition but were not added to ORS chapter 166 or any series therein. See Preface to Oregon Revised Statutes for further explanation.

166.433 Findings regarding transfers of firearms. The people of this state find that:

(1) The laws of Oregon regulating the sale of firearms contain a loophole that allows people other than gun dealers to sell firearms at gun shows without first conducting criminal background checks;

(2) It is necessary for the safety of the people of Oregon that any person who transfers a firearm at a gun show be required to request a criminal background check before completing the transfer of the firearm; and

(3) It is in the best interests of the people of Oregon that any person who transfers a firearm at any location other than a gun show be allowed to voluntarily request a criminal background check before completing the transfer of the firearm. [2001 c.1 §1]

Note: See note under 166.432.

166.434 Application of ORS 166.412 to all firearm transfers by gun dealers; fees for criminal background checks. (1) Notwithstanding the fact that ORS 166.412 requires a gun dealer to request a criminal history record check only when transferring a handgun, a gun dealer shall comply with the requirements of ORS 166.412 before transferring any firearm to a purchaser. The provisions of ORS 166.412 apply to the transfer of firearms other than handguns to the same extent that they apply to the transfer of handguns.

(2) In addition to the determination required by ORS 166.412 (3)(a)(A), in conducting a criminal background check or criminal history record check, the Department of State Police shall also determine whether the recipient is otherwise prohibited by state or federal law from possessing a firearm.

(3) Notwithstanding ORS 166.412 (5), the department is not required to operate the telephone number established under ORS 166.412 (5) on Thanksgiving Day or Christmas Day.

(4)(a) The department may charge a fee, not to exceed the amount authorized under ORS 166.414, for criminal background checks required under this section or ORS 166.436.

(b) The department shall establish a reduced fee for subsequent criminal background checks on the same recipient that are performed during the same day between the hours of 8 a.m. and 10 p.m. [2001 c.1 §5]

166.436 Firearm transfers by persons other than gun dealers; criminal background checks authorized; liability. (1) The Department of State Police shall make the telephone number established under ORS 166.412 (5) available for requests from persons other than gun dealers for criminal background checks under this section.

(2) Prior to transferring a firearm, a transferor other than a gun dealer may request by telephone that the department conduct a criminal background check on the recipient and shall provide the following information to the department:

(a) The name, address and telephone number of the transferor;

(b) The make, model, caliber and manufacturer's number of the firearm being transferred;

(c) The name, date of birth, race, sex and address of the recipient;

(d) The Social Security number of the recipient if the recipient voluntarily provides that number;

(e) The address of the place where the transfer is occurring; and

(f) The type, issuer and identification number of a current piece of identification bearing a recent photograph of the recipient presented by the recipient. The identification presented by the recipient must meet the requirements of ORS 166.412 (4)(a).

(3)(a) Upon receipt of a request for a criminal background check under this section, the department shall immediately, during the telephone call or by return call:

(A) Determine from criminal records and other information available to it whether the recipient is disqualified under ORS 166.470 from completing the transfer or is otherwise prohibited by state or federal law from possessing a firearm; and

(B) Notify the transferor when a recipient is disqualified from completing the transfer or provide the transferor with a unique approval number indicating that the recipient is qualified to complete the transfer. The unique approval number is a permit valid for 24 hours for the requested transfer. If the firearm is not transferred from the transferor to the recipient within 24 hours after receipt of the unique approval number, a new request must be made by the transferor.

(b) If the department is unable to determine whether the recipient is qualified for or disqualified from completing the transfer within 30 minutes of receiving the request, the department shall notify the transferor and provide the transferor with an estimate of the time when the department will provide the requested information.

(4) A public employee or public agency incurs no criminal or civil liability for performing the criminal background checks required by this section, provided the employee or agency acts in good faith and without malice.

(5)(a) The department may retain a record of the information obtained during a request for a criminal background check under this section for the period of time provided in ORS 166.412 (7).

(b) The record of the information obtained during a request for a criminal background check under this section is exempt from disclosure under public records law.

(6) The recipient of the firearm must be present when the transferor requests a criminal background check under this section.

(7)(a) Except as otherwise provided in paragraphs (b) and (c) of this subsection, a transferor who receives notification under this section that the recipient is qualified to complete the transfer of a firearm is immune from civil liability for any use of the firearm from the time of the transfer unless the transferor knows, or reasonably should know, that the recipient is likely to commit an unlawful act involving the firearm.

(b) If the transferor is required to request a criminal background check under ORS 166.438, the immunity provided by paragraph (a) of this subsection applies only if, in addition to receiving the notification required by this section, the transferor has the recipient fill out the form required by ORS 166.438 (1)(a) and retains the form as required by ORS 166.438 (2).

(c) The immunity provided by paragraph (a) of this subsection does not apply:

(A) If the transferor knows, or reasonably should know, that the recipient of the firearm intends to deliver the firearm to a third person who the transferor knows, or reasonably should know, may not lawfully possess the firearm; or

(B) In any product liability civil action under ORS 30.900 to 30.920. [2001 c.1 §6]

166.438 Transfer of firearms at gun shows.(1) A transferor other than a gun dealer may not transfer a firearm at a gun show unless the transferor:

(a)(A) Requests a criminal background check under ORS 166.436 prior to completing the transfer;
(B) Receives notification that the recipient is qualified to complete the transfer; and
(C) Has the recipient complete the form described in ORS 166.441; or
(b) Completes the transfer through a gun dealer.

(2) The transferor shall retain the completed form referred to in subsection (1) of this section for at least five years and shall make the completed form available to law enforcement agencies for the purpose of criminal investigations.

(3) A person who organizes a gun show shall post in a prominent place at the gun show a notice explaining the requirements of subsections (1) and (2) of this section. The person shall provide the form required by subsection (1) of this section to any person transferring a firearm at the gun show.

(4) Subsection (1) of this section does not apply if the transferee is licensed as a dealer under 18 U.S.C. 923.

(5)(a) Failure to comply with the requirements of subsection (1), (2) or (3) of this section is a Class A misdemeanor.
(b) Notwithstanding paragraph (a) of this subsection, failure to comply with the requirements of subsection (1), (2) or (3) of this section is a Class C felony if the person has two or more previous convictions under this section.

(6) It is an affirmative defense to a charge of violating subsection (1) or (3) of this section that the person did not know, or reasonably could not know, that more than 25 firearms were at the site and available for transfer. [2001 c.1 §7]

166.440 [Repealed by 1989 c.839 §39]

166.441 Form for transfer of firearm at gun show. (1) The Department of State Police shall develop a form to be completed by a person seeking to obtain a firearm at a gun show from a transferor other than a gun dealer. The department shall consider including in the form all of the requirements for disclosure of information that are required by federal law for over-the-counter firearms transactions.
(2) The department shall make the form available to the public at no cost. [2001 c.1 §8]

166.445 Short title. ORS 166.432 to 166.445 and the amendments to ORS 166.416, 166.418 and 166.460 by sections 9, 10 and 11, chapter 1, Oregon Laws 2001, shall be known as the Gun Violence Prevention Act. [2001 c.1 §2]

Note: See note under 166.432.

166.450 Obliteration or change of identification number on firearms. Any person who intentionally alters, removes or obliterates the identification number of any firearm for an unlawful purpose, shall be punished upon conviction by imprisonment in the custody of the Department of Corrections for not more than five years. Possession of any such firearm is presumptive evidence that the possessor has altered, removed or obliterated the identification number. [Amended by 1987 c.320 §90; 1989 c.839 §24]

166.460 Antique firearms excepted. (1) ORS 166.250, 166.260, 166.291 to 166.295, 166.410, 166.412, 166.425, 166.434, 166.438 and 166.450 do not apply to antique firearms.

(2) Notwithstanding the provisions of subsection (1) of this section, possession of an antique firearm by a person described in ORS 166.250 (1)(c)(B) to (D) or (F) constitutes a violation of ORS 166.250. [Amended by 1979 c.779 §6; 1989 c.839 §25; 1993 c.735 §8; 1995 c.729 §9; 2001 c.1 §11; 2001 c.666 §§35,47; 2003 c.614 §10; 2009 c.499 §5]

166.470 Limitations and conditions for sales of firearms. (1) Unless relief has been granted under ORS 166.274, 18 U.S.C. 925(c) or the expunction laws of this state or an equivalent law of another jurisdiction, a person may not intentionally sell, deliver or otherwise transfer any firearm when the transferor knows or reasonably should know that the recipient:

(a) Is under 18 years of age;

(b) Has been convicted of a felony;

(c) Has any outstanding felony warrants for arrest;

(d) Is free on any form of pretrial release for a felony;

(e) Was committed to the Oregon Health Authority under ORS 426.130;

(f) After January 1, 1990, was found to be mentally ill and subject to an order under ORS 426.130 that the person be prohibited from purchasing or possessing a firearm as a result of that mental illness;

(g) Has been convicted of a misdemeanor involving violence or found guilty except for insanity under ORS 161.295 of a misdemeanor involving violence within the previous four years. As used in this paragraph, "misdemeanor involving violence" means a misdemeanor described in ORS 163.160, 163.187, 163.190, 163.195 or 166.155 (1)(b); or

(h) Has been found guilty except for insanity under ORS 161.295 of a felony.

(2) A person may not sell, deliver or otherwise transfer any firearm that the person knows or reasonably should know is stolen.

(3) Subsection (1)(a) of this section does not prohibit:

(a) The parent or guardian, or another person with the consent of the parent or guardian, of a minor from transferring to the minor a firearm, other than a handgun; or

(b) The temporary transfer of any firearm to a minor for hunting, target practice or any other lawful purpose.

(4) Violation of this section is a Class A misdemeanor. [Amended by 1989 c.839 §3; 1991 c.67 §40; 1993 c.735 §11; 2001 c.828 §2; 2003 c.577 §7; 2009 c.499 §6; 2009 c.595 §115]

Note 1: The amendments to 166.470 by section 8, chapter 826, Oregon Laws 2009, become operative on the date that the rule described in section 13 (1), chapter 826, Oregon Laws 2009, is adopted by the Psychiatric Security Review Board. See section 13, chapter 826, Oregon Laws 2009, as amended by section 22, chapter 826, Oregon Laws 2009 (Note 4 under 166.274). The text that is operative from the date of adoption of that rule until January 2, 2012, is set forth for the user's convenience.

166.470. (1) Unless relief has been granted under ORS 166.274 or section 5, chapter 826, Oregon Laws 2009, or 18 U.S.C. 925(c) or the expunction laws of this state or an equivalent law of another jurisdiction, a person may not intentionally sell, deliver or otherwise transfer any firearm when the transferor knows or reasonably should know that the recipient:

(a) Is under 18 years of age;

(b) Has been convicted of a felony;

(c) Has any outstanding felony warrants for arrest;

(d) Is free on any form of pretrial release for a felony;

(e) Was committed to the Oregon Health Authority under ORS 426.130;

(f) After January 1, 1990, was found to be mentally ill and subject to an order under ORS 426.130 that the person be prohibited from purchasing or possessing a firearm as a result of that mental illness;

(g) Has been convicted of a misdemeanor involving violence or found guilty except for insanity under ORS 161.295 of a misdemeanor involving violence within the previous four years. As used in this paragraph, "misdemeanor involving violence" means a misdemeanor described in ORS 163.160, 163.187, 163.190, 163.195 or 166.155 (1)(b); or

(h) Has been found guilty except for insanity under ORS 161.295 of a felony.

(2) A person may not sell, deliver or otherwise transfer any firearm that the person knows or reasonably should know is stolen.

(3) Subsection (1)(a) of this section does not prohibit:

(a) The parent or guardian, or another person with the consent of the parent or guardian, of a minor from transferring to the minor a firearm, other than a handgun; or

(b) The temporary transfer of any firearm to a minor for hunting, target practice or any other lawful purpose.

(4) Violation of this section is a Class A misdemeanor.

Note 2: The amendments to 166.470 by section 11, chapter 826, Oregon Laws 2009, become operative January 2, 2012. See section 14, chapter 826, Oregon Laws 2009, as amended by section 23, chapter 826, Oregon Laws 2009. The text that is operative on and after January 2, 2012, is set forth for the user's convenience.

166.470. (1) Unless relief has been granted under ORS 166.274 or 18 U.S.C. 925(c) or the expunction laws of this state or an equivalent law of another jurisdiction, a person may not intentionally sell, deliver or otherwise transfer any firearm when the transferor knows or reasonably should know that the recipient:

(a) Is under 18 years of age;

(b) Has been convicted of a felony;

(c) Has any outstanding felony warrants for arrest;

(d) Is free on any form of pretrial release for a felony;

(e) Was committed to the Oregon Health Authority under ORS 426.130;

(f) After January 1, 1990, was found to be mentally ill and subject to an order under ORS 426.130 that the person be prohibited from purchasing or possessing a firearm as a result of that mental illness;

(g) Has been convicted of a misdemeanor involving violence or found guilty except for insanity under ORS 161.295 of a misdemeanor involving violence within the previous four years. As used in this paragraph, "misdemeanor involving violence" means a misdemeanor described in ORS 163.160, 163.187, 163.190, 163.195 or

166.155 (1)(b); or
(h) Has been found guilty except for insanity under ORS
161.295 of a felony.
(2) A person may not sell, deliver or otherwise transfer any
firearm that the person knows or reasonably should know is
stolen.
(3) Subsection (1)(a) of this section does not prohibit:
(a) The parent or guardian, or another person with the
consent of the parent or guardian, of a minor from transferring to the minor a firearm, other than a handgun; or
(b) The temporary transfer of any firearm to a minor for
hunting, target practice or any other lawful purpose.
(4) Violation of this section is a Class A misdemeanor.

166.480 **Sale or gift of explosives to children.** Any person who
sells, exchanges, barters or gives to any child, under the age
of 14 years, any explosive article or substance, other than an
ordinary firecracker containing not more than 10 grains of
gunpowder or who sells, exchanges, barters or gives to any
such child, any instrument or apparatus, the chief utility of
which is the fact that it is used, or is ordinarily capable of being
used, as an article or device to increase the force or intensity
of any explosive, or to direct or control the discharge of any
such explosive, is guilty of a misdemeanor. [Amended by 1989
c.839 §26]

166.490 **Purchase of firearms in certain other states.** (1) As used in
this section, unless the context requires otherwise:
(a) "Contiguous state" means California, Idaho, Nevada or
Washington.
(b) "Resident" includes an individual or a corporation or
other business entity that maintains a place of business in
this state.
(2) A resident of this state may purchase or otherwise obtain a
rifle or shotgun in a contiguous state and receive in this state
or transport into this state such rifle or shotgun, unless the
purchase or transfer violates the law of this state, the state in
which the purchase or transfer is made or the United States.
(3) This section does not apply to the purchase, receipt or
transportation of rifles and shotguns by federally licensed
firearms manufacturers, importers, dealers or collectors.
(4) This section expires and stands repealed upon the date
that section 922(b) (3) of the Gun Control Act of 1968 (18
U.S.C. 922(b) (3)) and regulations pursuant thereto are
repealed or rescinded. [1969 c.289 §§1,2,3,4]

166.510 [Amended by 1957 c.290 §1; 1973 c.746 §1; 1983 c.546 §2; repealed by 1985 c.709 §4]

166.515 [1973 c.746 §2; repealed by 1985 c.709 §4]

166.520 [Amended by 1973 c.746 §3; repealed by 1985 c.709 §4]

166.560 [1965 c.118 §1; repealed by 1971 c.743 §432]

166.610 [Repealed by 1971 c.743 §432]

166.620 [Repealed by 1963 c.94 §2]

DISCHARGING WEAPONS

166.630 Discharging weapon on or across highway, ocean shore recreation area or public utility facility. (1) Except as provided in ORS 166.220, any person is guilty of a violation who discharges or attempts to discharge any blowgun, bow and arrow, crossbow, air rifle or firearm:

(a) Upon or across any highway, railroad right of way or other public road in this state, or upon or across the ocean shore within the state recreation area as defined in ORS 390.605.

(b) At any public or railroad sign or signal or an electric power, communication, petroleum or natural gas transmission or distribution facility of a public utility, telecommunications utility or railroad within range of the weapon.

(2) Any blowgun, bow and arrow, crossbow, air rifle or firearm in the possession of the person that was used in committing a violation of this section may be confiscated and forfeited to the State of Oregon. This section does not prevent:

(a) The discharge of firearms by peace officers in the performance of their duty or by military personnel within the confines of a military reservation.

(b) The discharge of firearms by an employee of the United States Department of Agriculture acting within the scope of employment in the course of the lawful taking of wildlife.

(3) The hunting license revocation provided in ORS 497.415 is in addition to and not in lieu of the penalty and forfeiture provided in subsections (1) and (2) of this section.

(4) As used in this section:

(a) "Public sign" includes all signs, signals and markings placed or erected by authority of a public body.

(b) "Public utility" has the meaning given that term in ORS 164.365 (2).
(c) "Railroad" has the meaning given that term in ORS 824.020. [Amended by 1963 c.94 §1; 1969 c.501 §2; 1969 c.511 §4; 1973 c.196 §1; 1973 c.723 §118; 1981 c.900 §1; 1987 c.447 §113; 1991 c.797 §2; 2009 c.556 §7]

166.635 Discharging weapon or throwing objects at trains. (1) A person shall not knowingly throw an object at, drop an object on, or discharge a bow and arrow, air rifle, rifle, gun, revolver or other firearm at a railroad train, a person on a railroad train or a commodity being transported on a railroad train. This subsection does not prevent a peace officer or a railroad employee from performing the duty of a peace officer or railroad employee.
(2) Violation of subsection (1) of this section is a misdemeanor. [1973 c.139 §4]

166.638 Discharging weapon across airport operational surfaces. (1) Any person who knowingly or recklessly discharges any bow and arrow, gun, air gun or other firearm upon or across any airport operational surface commits a Class A misdemeanor. Any bow and arrow, gun, air gun or other firearm in the possession of the person that was used in committing a violation of this subsection may be confiscated and forfeited to the State of Oregon, and the clear proceeds shall be deposited with the State Treasury in the Common School Fund.
(2) As used in subsection (1) of this section, "airport operational surface" means any surface of land or water developed, posted or marked so as to give an observer reasonable notice that the surface is developed for the purpose of storing, parking, taxiing or operating aircraft, or any surface of land or water when actually being used for such purpose.
(3) Subsection (1) of this section does not prohibit the discharge of firearms by peace officers in the performance of their duty or by military personnel within the confines of a military reservation, or otherwise lawful hunting, wildlife control or other discharging of firearms done with the consent of the proprietor, manager or custodian of the airport operational surface.
(4) The hunting license revocation provided in ORS 497.415 is in addition to and not in lieu of the penalty provided in subsection (1) of this section. [1981 c.901 §2; 1987 c.858 §2]

166.640 [Repealed by 1971 c.743 §432]

POSSESSION OF BODY ARMOR

166.641 Definitions for ORS 166.641 to 166.643. As used in this section and ORS 166.642 and 166.643:

(1) "Body armor" means any clothing or equipment designed in whole or in part to minimize the risk of injury from a deadly weapon.

(2) "Deadly weapon" has the meaning given that term in ORS 161.015.

(3) "Misdemeanor involving violence" has the meaning given that term in ORS 166.470. [2001 c.635 §1]

166.642 Felon in possession of body armor. (1) A person commits the crime of felon in possession of body armor if the person:

(a) Has been convicted of a felony or misdemeanor involving violence under the law of any state or the United States; and

(b) Knowingly is in possession or control of body armor.

(2) Felon in possession of body armor is a Class C felony.

(3) For purposes of subsection (1) of this section, a person who has been found to be within the jurisdiction of a juvenile court for having committed an act that would constitute a felony or misdemeanor involving violence has been convicted of a felony or misdemeanor involving violence.

(4) Subsection (1) of this section does not apply to:

(a) A person who is wearing body armor provided by a peace officer for the person's safety or protection while the person is being transported or accompanied by a peace officer; or

(b) A person who has been convicted of only one felony under the law of this state or any other state, or who has been convicted of only one felony under the law of the United States, which felony did not involve criminal homicide, as defined in ORS 163.005, and who has been discharged from imprisonment, parole or probation for the offense for a period of 15 years prior to the date of the alleged violation of subsection (1) of this section.

(5) It is an affirmative defense to a charge of violating subsection (1) of this section that a protective order or restraining order has been entered to the benefit of the person. The affirmative defense created by this subsection is not available if the person possesses the body armor while committing or attempting to commit a crime. [2001 c.635 §2]

166.643 Unlawful possession of body armor. (1) A person commits the crime of unlawful possession of body armor if the person, while committing or attempting to commit a felony or misdemeanor involving violence, knowingly:
(a) Wears body armor; and
(b) Possesses a deadly weapon.
(2) Unlawful possession of body armor is a Class B felony. [2001 c.635 §3]

MISCELLANEOUS

166.645 Hunting in cemeteries prohibited. (1) Hunting in cemeteries is prohibited.
(2) As used in subsection (1) of this section "hunting" has the meaning for that term provided in ORS 496.004.
(3) Violation of subsection (1) of this section is a misdemeanor. [1973 c.468 §2; 1987 c.158 §30]

166.649 Throwing an object off an overpass in the second degree. (1) A person commits the crime of throwing an object off an overpass in the second degree if the person:
(a) With criminal negligence throws an object off an overpass; and
(b) Knows, or reasonably should have known, that the object was of a type or size to cause damage to any person or vehicle that the object might hit.
(2) Throwing an object off an overpass in the second degree is a Class A misdemeanor.
(3) As used in this section and ORS 166.651, "overpass" means a structure carrying a roadway or pedestrian pathway over a roadway. [1993 c.731 §1]

166.650 [Repealed by 1971 c.743 §432]

166.651 Throwing an object off an overpass in the first degree. (1) A person commits the crime of throwing an object off an overpass in the first degree if the person:
(a) Recklessly throws an object off an overpass; and
(b) Knows, or reasonably should have known, that the object was of a type or size to cause damage to any person or vehicle that the object might hit.
(2) Throwing an object off an overpass in the first degree is a Class C felony. [1993 c.731 §2]

166.660 Unlawful paramilitary activity. (1) A person commits the crime of unlawful paramilitary activity if the person:

(a) Exhibits, displays or demonstrates to another person the use, application or making of any firearm, explosive or incendiary device or any technique capable of causing injury or death to persons and intends or knows that such firearm, explosive or incendiary device or technique will be unlawfully employed for use in a civil disorder; or

(b) Assembles with one or more other persons for the purpose of training with, practicing with or being instructed in the use of any firearm, explosive or incendiary device or technique capable of causing injury or death to persons with the intent to unlawfully employ such firearm, explosive or incendiary device or technique in a civil disorder.

(2)(a) Nothing in this section makes unlawful any act of any law enforcement officer performed in the otherwise lawful performance of the officer's official duties.

(b) Nothing in this section makes unlawful any activity of the State Department of Fish and Wildlife, or any activity intended to teach or practice self-defense or self-defense techniques, such as karate clubs or self-defense clinics, and similar lawful activity, or any facility, program or lawful activity related to firearms instruction and training intended to teach the safe handling and use of firearms, or any other lawful sports or activities related to the individual recreational use or possession of firearms, including but not limited to hunting activities, target shooting, self-defense, firearms collection or any organized activity including, but not limited to any hunting club, rifle club, rifle range or shooting range which does not include a conspiracy as defined in ORS 161.450 or the knowledge of or the intent to cause or further a civil disorder.

(3) Unlawful paramilitary activity is a Class C felony.

(4) As used in this section:

(a) "Civil disorder" means acts of physical violence by assemblages of three or more persons which cause damage or injury, or immediate danger thereof, to the person or property of any other individual.

(b) "Firearm" has the meaning given that term in ORS 166.210.

(c) "Explosive" means a chemical compound, mixture or device that is commonly used or intended for the purpose of producing a chemical reaction resulting in a substantially instantaneous release of gas and heat, including but not limited to dynamite, blasting powder, nitroglycerin, blasting caps and nitrojelly, but excluding fireworks as defined in ORS 480.110 (1), black powder, smokeless powder, small arms ammunition and small arms ammunition primers.

(d) "Law enforcement officer" means any duly constituted police officer of the United States, any state, any political subdivision of a state or the District of Columbia, and also includes members of the military reserve forces or National Guard as defined in 10 U.S.C. 101 (9), members of the organized militia of any state or territory of the United States, the Commonwealth of Puerto Rico or the District of Columbia not included within the definition of National Guard as defined by 10 U.S.C. 101 (9), members of the Armed Forces of the United States and such persons as are defined in ORS 161.015 (4) when in the performance of official duties. [1983 c.792 §2; 1987 c.858 §3; 2001 c.666 §§26,38; 2005 c.830 §27; 2009 c.610 §7]

166.663 Casting artificial light from vehicle while possessing certain weapons prohibited. (1) A person may not cast from a motor vehicle an artificial light while there is in the possession or in the immediate physical presence of the person a bow and arrow or a rifle, gun, revolver or other firearm.

(2) Subsection (1) of this section does not apply to a person casting an artificial light:

(a) From the headlights of a motor vehicle that is being operated on a road in the usual manner.

(b) When the bow and arrow, rifle, gun, revolver or other firearm that the person has in the possession or immediate physical presence of the person is disassembled or stored, or in the trunk or storage compartment of the motor vehicle.

(c) When the ammunition or arrows are stored separate from the weapon.

(d) On land owned or lawfully occupied by that person.

(e) On publicly owned land when that person has an agreement with the public body to use that property.

(f) When the person is a peace officer or government employee engaged in the performance of official duties.

(g) When the person has been issued a license under ORS 166.291 and 166.292 to carry a concealed weapon.

(3) A peace officer may issue a citation to a person for a violation of subsection (1) of this section when the violation is committed

in the presence of the peace officer or when the peace officer has probable cause to believe that a violation has occurred based on a description of the vehicle or other information received from a peace officer who observed the violation.
(4) Violation of subsection (1) of this section is punishable as a Class B violation.
(5) As used in this section, "peace officer" has the meaning given that term in ORS 161.015. [1989 c.848 §2; 1999 c.1051 §159; 2005 c.22 §116; 2009 c.610 §3]

166.710 [1957 c.601 §1; repealed by 1971 c.743 §432]

USE OF FORCE STATUTES

161.195 "Justification" described. (1) Unless inconsistent with other provisions of chapter 743, Oregon Laws 1971, defining justifiable use of physical force, or with some other provision of law, conduct which would otherwise constitute an offense is justifiable and not criminal when it is required or authorized by law or by a judicial decree or is performed by a public servant in the reasonable exercise of official powers, duties or functions.
(2) As used in subsection (1) of this section, "laws and judicial decrees" include but are not limited to:
   (a) Laws defining duties and functions of public servants;
   (b) Laws defining duties of private citizens to assist public servants in the performance of certain of their functions;
   (c) Laws governing the execution of legal process;
   (d) Laws governing the military services and conduct of war; and
   (e) Judgments and orders of courts. [1971 c.743 §19]

Note: See note under 161.015.

161.200 Choice of evils. (1) Unless inconsistent with other provisions of chapter 743, Oregon Laws 1971, defining justifiable use of physical force, or with some other provision of law, conduct which would otherwise constitute an offense is justifiable and not criminal when:
   (a) That conduct is necessary as an emergency measure to avoid an imminent public or private injury; and
   (b) The threatened injury is of such gravity that, according to ordinary standards of intelligence and morality, the desirability and urgency of avoiding the injury clearly outweigh

the desirability of avoiding the injury sought to be prevented by the statute defining the offense in issue.

(2) The necessity and justifiability of conduct under subsection (1) of this section shall not rest upon considerations pertaining only to the morality and advisability of the statute, either in its general application or with respect to its application to a particular class of cases arising thereunder. [1971 c.743 §20]

Note: See note under 161.015.

161.205 Use of physical force generally. The use of physical force upon another person that would otherwise constitute an offense is justifiable and not criminal under any of the following circumstances:

(1) A parent, guardian or other person entrusted with the care and supervision of a minor or an incompetent person may use reasonable physical force upon such minor or incompetent person when and to the extent the person reasonably believes it necessary to maintain discipline or to promote the welfare of the minor or incompetent person. A teacher may use reasonable physical force upon a student when and to the extent the teacher reasonably believes it necessary to maintain order in the school or classroom or at a school activity or event, whether or not it is held on school property.

(2) An authorized official of a jail, prison or correctional facility may use physical force when and to the extent that the official reasonably believes it necessary to maintain order and discipline or as is authorized by law.

(3) A person responsible for the maintenance of order in a common carrier of passengers, or a person acting under the direction of the person, may use physical force when and to the extent that the person reasonably believes it necessary to maintain order, but the person may use deadly physical force only when the person reasonably believes it necessary to prevent death or serious physical injury.

(4) A person acting under a reasonable belief that another person is about to commit suicide or to inflict serious physical self-injury may use physical force upon that person to the extent that the person reasonably believes it necessary to thwart the result.

(5) A person may use physical force upon another person in self-defense or in defending a third person, in defending property, in making an arrest or in preventing an escape, as hereafter prescribed in chapter 743, Oregon Laws 1971. [1971 c.743 §21; 1981 c.246 §1]

Note: See note under 161.015.

161.209 Use of physical force in defense of a person. Except as provided in ORS 161.215 and 161.219, a person is justified in using physical force upon another person for self-defense or to defend a third person from what the person reasonably believes to be the use or imminent use of unlawful physical force, and the person may use a degree of force which the person reasonably believes to be necessary for the purpose. [1971 c.743 §22]

161.210 [Repealed by 1971 c.743 §432]

161.215 Limitations on use of physical force in defense of a person. Notwithstanding ORS 161.209, a person is not justified in using physical force upon another person if:
(1) With intent to cause physical injury or death to another person, the person provokes the use of unlawful physical force by that person; or
(2) The person is the initial aggressor, except that the use of physical force upon another person under such circumstances is justifiable if the person withdraws from the encounter and effectively communicates to the other person the intent to do so, but the latter nevertheless continues or threatens to continue the use of unlawful physical force; or
(3) The physical force involved is the product of a combat by agreement not specifically authorized by law. [1971 c.743 §24]

161.219 Limitations on use of deadly physical force in defense of a person. Notwithstanding the provisions of ORS 161.209, a person is not justified in using deadly physical force upon another person unless the person reasonably believes that the other person is:
(1) Committing or attempting to commit a felony involving the use or threatened imminent use of physical force against a person; or
(2) Committing or attempting to commit a burglary in a dwelling; or
(3) Using or about to use unlawful deadly physical force against a person. [1971 c.743 §23]

161.220 [Repealed by 1971 c.743 §432]

161.225 Use of physical force in defense of premises. (1) A person in lawful possession or control of premises is justified in using physical force upon another person when and to the extent that the person reasonably believes it necessary to prevent or terminate what the person reasonably believes to be the commission or attempted commission of a criminal trespass by the other person in or upon the premises.

(2) A person may use deadly physical force under the circumstances set forth in subsection (1) of this section only:

(a) In defense of a person as provided in ORS 161.219; or

(b) When the person reasonably believes it necessary to prevent the commission of arson or a felony by force and violence by the trespasser.

(3) As used in subsection (1) and subsection (2)(a) of this section, "premises" includes any building as defined in ORS 164.205 and any real property. As used in subsection (2)(b) of this section, "premises" includes any building. [1971 c.743 §25]

161.229 Use of physical force in defense of property. A person is justified in using physical force, other than deadly physical force, upon another person when and to the extent that the person reasonably believes it to be necessary to prevent or terminate the commission or attempted commission by the other person of theft or criminal mischief of property. [1971 c.743 §26]

161.230 [Repealed by 1971 c.743 §432]

161.235 Use of physical force in making an arrest or in preventing an escape. Except as provided in ORS 161.239, a peace officer is justified in using physical force upon another person only when and to the extent that the peace officer reasonably believes it necessary:

(1) To make an arrest or to prevent the escape from custody of an arrested person unless the peace officer knows that the arrest is unlawful; or

(2) For self-defense or to defend a third person from what the peace officer reasonably believes to be the use or imminent use of physical force while making or attempting to make an arrest or while preventing or attempting to prevent an escape. [1971 c.743 §27]

161.239 Use of deadly physical force in making an arrest or in preventing an escape. (1) Notwithstanding the provisions of ORS 161.235, a peace officer may use deadly physical force only when the peace officer reasonably believes that:

(a) The crime committed by the person was a felony or an attempt to commit a felony involving the use or threatened imminent use of physical force against a person; or

(b) The crime committed by the person was kidnapping, arson, escape in the first degree, burglary in the first degree or any attempt to commit such a crime; or

(c) Regardless of the particular offense which is the subject of the arrest or attempted escape, the use of deadly physical force is necessary to defend the peace officer or another person from the use or threatened imminent use of deadly physical force; or

(d) The crime committed by the person was a felony or an attempt to commit a felony and under the totality of the circumstances existing at the time and place, the use of such force is necessary; or

(e) The officer's life or personal safety is endangered in the particular circumstances involved.

(2) Nothing in subsection (1) of this section constitutes justification for reckless or criminally negligent conduct by a peace officer amounting to an offense against or with respect to innocent persons whom the peace officer is not seeking to arrest or retain in custody. [1971 c.743 §28]

161.240 [Repealed by 1971 c.743 §432]

161.245 "Reasonable belief" described; status of unlawful arrest. (1) For the purposes of ORS 161.235 and 161.239, a reasonable belief that a person has committed an offense means a reasonable belief in facts or circumstances which if true would in law constitute an offense. If the believed facts or circumstances would not in law constitute an offense, an erroneous though not unreasonable belief that the law is otherwise does not render justifiable the use of force to make an arrest or to prevent an escape from custody.

(2) A peace officer who is making an arrest is justified in using the physical force prescribed in ORS 161.235 and 161.239 unless the arrest is unlawful and is known by the officer to be unlawful. [1971 c.743 §29]

161.249 Use of physical force by private person assisting an arrest. (1) Except as provided in subsection (2) of this section, a person who has been directed by a peace officer to assist the peace officer to make an arrest or to prevent an escape from custody is justified in using physical force when and to the extent that the person reasonably believes that force to be necessary to carry out the peace officer's direction.

(2) A person who has been directed to assist a peace officer under circumstances specified in subsection (1) of this section may use deadly physical force to make an arrest or to prevent an escape only when:

    (a) The person reasonably believes that force to be necessary for self-defense or to defend a third person from what the person reasonably believes to be the use or imminent use of deadly physical force; or

    (b) The person is directed or authorized by the peace officer to use deadly physical force unless the person knows that the peace officer is not authorized to use deadly physical force under the circumstances. [1971 c.743 §30]

161.250 [Repealed by 1971 c.743 §432]

161.255 Use of physical force by private person making citizen's arrest. (1) Except as provided in subsection (2) of this section, a private person acting on the person's own account is justified in using physical force upon another person when and to the extent that the person reasonably believes it necessary to make an arrest or to prevent the escape from custody of an arrested person whom the person has arrested under ORS 133.225.

(2) A private person acting under the circumstances prescribed in subsection (1) of this section is justified in using deadly physical force only when the person reasonably believes it necessary for self-defense or to defend a third person from what the person reasonably believes to be the use or imminent use of deadly physical force. [1971 c.743 §31; 1973 c.836 §339]

161.260 Use of physical force in resisting arrest prohibited. A person may not use physical force to resist an arrest by a peace officer who is known or reasonably appears to be a peace officer, whether the arrest is lawful or unlawful. [1971 c.743 §32]

161.265 Use of physical force to prevent escape. (1) A guard or other peace officer employed in a correctional facility, as that term is defined in ORS 162.135, is justified in using physical force, including deadly physical force, when and to the extent that the guard or peace officer reasonably believes it necessary to prevent the escape of a prisoner from a correctional facility.

(2) Notwithstanding subsection (1) of this section, a guard or other peace officer employed by the Department of Corrections may not use deadly physical force in the circumstances described in ORS 161.267 (3). [1971 c.743 §33; 2005 c.431 §3]

161.267 **Use of physical force by corrections officer or official employed by Department of Corrections.** (1) As used in this section:

(a) "Colocated minimum security facility" means a Department of Corrections institution that has been designated by the Department of Corrections as a minimum security facility and has been located by the department on the grounds of a medium or higher security Department of Corrections institution.

(b) "Department of Corrections institution" has the meaning given that term in ORS 421.005.

(c) "Stand-alone minimum security facility" means a Department of Corrections institution that has been designated by the department as a minimum security facility and that has been located by the department separate and apart from other Department of Corrections institutions.

(2) A corrections officer or other official employed by the Department of Corrections is justified in using physical force, including deadly physical force, when and to the extent that the officer or official reasonably believes it necessary to:

(a) Prevent the escape of an inmate from a Department of Corrections institution, including the grounds of the institution, or from custody;

(b) Maintain or restore order and discipline in a Department of Corrections institution, or any part of the institution, in the event of a riot, disturbance or other occurrence that threatens the safety of inmates, department employees or other persons; or

(c) Prevent serious physical injury to or the death of the officer, official or another person.

(3) Notwithstanding subsection (2)(a) of this section, a corrections officer or other official employed by the department may not use deadly physical force to prevent the escape of an inmate from:

(a) A stand-alone minimum security facility;

(b) A colocated minimum security facility, if the corrections officer or other official knows that the inmate has been classified by the department as minimum custody; or

(c) Custody outside of a Department of Corrections institution:

(A) While the inmate is assigned to an inmate work crew; or

(B) During transport or other supervised activity, if the inmate is classified by the department as minimum custody and the inmate is not being transported or supervised with an inmate who has been classified by the department as medium or higher custody.

(4) Nothing in this section limits the authority of a person to use physical force under ORS 161.205 (2) or 161.265. [2005 c.431 §2]

161.270 Duress. (1) The commission of acts which would otherwise constitute an offense, other than murder, is not criminal if the actor engaged in the proscribed conduct because the actor was coerced to do so by the use or threatened use of unlawful physical force upon the actor or a third person, which force or threatened force was of such nature or degree to overcome earnest resistance.

(2) Duress is not a defense for one who intentionally or recklessly places oneself in a situation in which it is probable that one will be subjected to duress.

(3) It is not a defense that a spouse acted on the command of the other spouse, unless the spouse acted under such coercion as would establish a defense under subsection (1) of this section. [1971 c.743 §34; 1987 c.158 §22]

IREGORY A. CHAIMOV
LEGISLATIVE COUNSEL

900 COURT ST NE S101
SALEM OR 97301-4065
(503) 986-1243
FAX (503) 373-1043
www.lc.state.or.us

STATE OF OREGON
LEGISLATIVE COUNSEL COMMITTEE
March 15, 2004

Representative Wayne Scott
House Majority Leader
P.O. Box 664
Canby, Oregon 97013

Re: Authority of Port of Portland to regulate firearm possession

Dear Representative Scott:

You ask whether the Port of Portland has the authority to enact regulations prohibiting a person from carrying a firearm in the terminal at Portland International Airport.

The short answer is no.

Discussion

In 1995 and 1997, the legislature enacted a series of statutes that vested solely in the Legislative Assembly the authority to regulate matters relating to firearms, while granting limited authority to counties and cities to regulate very specific aspects of firearm use and possession. See ORS 166.170 to 166.176. The statute of primary importance to your inquiry is ORS 166.170.

ORS 174.020 (1)(a) provides that "[i]n the construction of a statute, a court shall pursue the intention of the legislature if possible." The Oregon Supreme Court, in Portland General Electric v. Bureau of Labor and Industries, 317 Or. 606 (1993), set out a three-level process to analyze a statute to determine legislative intent. The first level of analysis is to examine the text and context of a statute. Id. at 610. The starting point for the first level is the text of the specific statutory provision because it "is the best evidence of the legislature's intent." Id.

In attempting to determine the meaning of the statutory provision, the court may also consider rules of statutory construction that directly relate to how to read the text. These rules may be found in statutes or in case law. Id. at 611. In addition, the court may, at this first level, examine the context of the statute including related statutes. Id.

Under Portland General Electric, if one can determine the legislature's intent from the analysis described above, no further inquiry is necessary or allowed. Only if the intent remains unclear after the first level can one move to the second level of analysis, which is consideration of the legislative history of the statutory provision.[1] Id. at 611-612; Young v. State, 161 Or. App.

_____

[1] In 2001, the Legislative Assembly amended ORS 174.020 to expressly allow parties to offer legislative history to "assist a court in its construction of a statute." ORS 174.020 (1)(b). The amendments further provided that the court could limit consideration of legislative history to information provided by the parties and directed courts to "give the weight to the legislative history that the court considers to be appropriate." ORS 174.020 (3). It is not clear if the effect of the 2001 amendments is to allow courts to consider legislative history at the first level of analysis under Portland General Electric. See Smith v. Salem-Keizer School District and Fair Dismissal Appeals Board, 188 Or. App. 237, 245 (2003) and Stevens v. Czerniak, 336 Or. 392, n.12 (2004).

Representative Wayne Scott
March 15, 2004
Page 2

32, 37-38 (1999). The third and final level of analysis, which can be reached only after going through the first two levels, is consideration of general maxims of statutory construction. Portland General Electric at 612.

Using the framework for statutory construction set out in Portland General Electric to determine what the legislature intended in enacting ORS 166.170, we begin by looking at the text of the statute itself. ORS 166.170 provides:

> 166.170. (1) Except as expressly authorized by state statute, the authority to regulate in any matter whatsoever the sale, acquisition, transfer, ownership, possession, storage, transportation or use of firearms or any element relating to firearms and components thereof, including ammunition, is vested solely in the Legislative Assembly.
>
> (2) Except as expressly authorized by state statute, no county, city or other municipal corporation or district may enact civil or criminal ordinances, including but not limited to zoning ordinances, to regulate, restrict or prohibit the sale, acquisition, transfer, ownership, possession, storage, transportation or use of firearms or any element relating to firearms and components thereof, including ammunition. Ordinances that are contrary to this subsection are void.

By its plain terms, subsection (1) of the statute vests exclusively in the Legislative Assembly the authority to regulate all of the listed activities and things related to firearms. Subsection (2) of the statute goes on to specifically prohibit counties, cities and other municipal corporations and districts from enacting civil or criminal ordinances regulating the same activities and things related to firearms. The only exception to the preemption of subsection (1) and the prohibition in subsection (2) is through express authorization by state statute. For authority to be express it must be explicitly stated that the entity can exercise some sort of regulatory authority over firearms. Therefore, unless there is a statute that explicitly says that some entity may regulate firearms in some manner, it may not do so.

ORS 166.171 to 166.176 are examples of such express grants of authority. ORS 166.173 authorizes cities and counties to adopt ordinances to regulate the possession of loaded firearms in public places. The statute also provides that such an ordinance does not apply to or affect certain listed persons, including a person licensed to carry a concealed handgun.

For purposes of your inquiry, one should note that ORS 166.170 (2) specifically includes districts within its prohibition. It is also important to note that the express authority granted by

---

ORS 174.020 provides:

> 174.020. (1)(a) In the construction of a statute, a court shall pursue the intention of the legislature if possible.
> (b) To assist a court in its construction of a statute, a party may offer the legislative history of the statute.
> (2) When a general and particular provision are inconsistent, the latter is paramount to the former so that a particular intent controls a general intent that is inconsistent with the particular intent.
> (3) A court may limit its consideration of legislative history to the information that the parties provide to the court. A court shall give the weight to the legislative history that the court considers to be appropriate.

K:\oprnus\00135 vrv.doc

Representative Wayne Scott
March 15, 2004
Page 3

ORS 166.173 to regulate possession of loaded firearms in public places is given only to cities and counties and not to districts.

The Port of Portland is a district. ORS 778.010 provides that "[t]he Portland metropolitan area is a separate district, to be known as the Port of Portland. . . ." Because "district" is not defined for purposes of ORS 166.170, the term must be given its ordinary meaning and would include the Port of Portland.

Although the Port of Portland is given general authority to make regulations "to provide for policing or regulating the use of airports, and any facilities located at or in conjunction with airports, owned, operated, maintained or controlled by the port," ORS 778.260, the statute does not contain express authority to regulate firearms. ORS 778.260 does not mention firearms. At best, one could argue that such authority could be implied from the statute; however, implied authority is not express authority and therefore is not sufficient under ORS 166.170.

Because the port lacks the express statutory authority to regulate firearms required by ORS 166.170 (1), it may not enact regulations prohibiting a person from carrying a firearm at Portland International Airport.

The opinions written by the Legislative Counsel and the staff of the Legislative Counsel's office are prepared solely for the purpose of assisting members of the Legislative Assembly in the development and consideration of legislative matters. In performing their duties, the Legislative Counsel and the members of the staff of the Legislative Counsel's office have no authority to provide legal advice to any other person, group or entity. For this reason, this opinion should not be considered or used as legal advice by any person other than legislators in the conduct of legislative business. Public bodies and their officers and employees should seek and rely upon the advice and opinion of the Attorney General, district attorney, county counsel, city attorney or other retained counsel. Constituents and other private persons and entities should seek and rely upon the advice and opinion of private counsel.

Very truly yours,

GREGORY A. CHAIMOV
Legislative Counsel

By

Virginia R. Vanderbilt
Senior Deputy Legislative Counsel

GREGORY A. CHAIMOV
LEGISLATIVE COUNSEL

900 COURT ST NE S 101
SALEM OR 97301-4065
(503) 986-1243
FAX (503) 373-1043
www.lc.state.or.us

STATE OF OREGON
LEGISLATIVE COUNSEL COMMITTEE

March 10, 2004

Representative Wayne Krieger
95702 Skyview Ranch Road
Gold Beach, Oregon 97444

Re: Regulation of weapons at educational institutions

Dear Representative Krieger:

You ask whether elementary and secondary schools, community colleges and institutions within the Oregon University System have the authority to prohibit a person from carrying a permitted weapon on the campus of such schools, colleges and institutions. The short answer is no as your inquiry relates to firearms, although this conclusion is not free from doubt, and yes as to other weapons.

Discussion

In answering your inquiry, we assumed that by "permitted weapon" you mean a weapon that the person is not otherwise prohibited by state or federal law from possessing.

1. Firearms

In 1995 and 1997, the legislature enacted a series of statutes that vested solely in the Legislative Assembly the authority to regulate matters relating to firearms, while granting limited authority to counties and cities to regulate very specific aspects of firearm use and possession. See ORS 166.170 to 166.176. The statute of primary importance to your inquiry is ORS 166.170.

ORS 174.020 (1)(a) provides that "[i]n the construction of a statute, a court shall pursue the intention of the legislature if possible." The Oregon Supreme Court, in Portland General Electric v. Bureau of Labor and Industries, 317 Or. 606 (1993), set out a three-level process to analyze a statute to determine legislative intent. The first level of analysis is to examine the text and context of a statute. Id. at 610. The starting point for the first level is the text of the specific statutory provision because it "is the best evidence of the legislature's intent." Id.

In attempting to determine the meaning of the statutory provision, the court may also consider rules of statutory construction that directly relate to how to read the text. These rules may be found in statutes or in case law. Id. at 611. In addition, the court may, at this first level, examine the context of the statute including related statutes. Id.

Under Portland General Electric, if one can determine the legislature's intent from the analysis described above, no further inquiry is necessary or allowed. Only if the intent remains unclear after the first level can one move to the second level of analysis, which is consideration of the legislative history of the statutory provision.[1] Id. at 611-612; Young v. State, 161 Or. App. 32, 37-38 (1999). The third and final level of analysis, which can be reached only after going through the first two levels, is consideration of general maxims of statutory construction. Portland General Electric at 612.

Using the framework for statutory construction set out in Portland General Electric to determine what the legislature intended in enacting ORS 166.170, we begin by looking at the text of the statute itself. ORS 166.170 provides:

> 166.170 (1) Except as expressly authorized by state statute, the authority to regulate in any matter whatsoever the sale, acquisition, transfer, ownership, possession, storage, transportation or use of firearms or any element relating to firearms and components thereof, including ammunition, is vested solely in the Legislative Assembly.
>
> (2) Except as expressly authorized by state statute, no county, city or other municipal corporation or district may enact civil or criminal ordinances, including but not limited to zoning ordinances, to regulate, restrict or prohibit the sale, acquisition, transfer, ownership, possession, storage, transportation or use of firearms or any element relating to firearms and components thereof, including ammunition. Ordinances that are contrary to this subsection are void.

By its plain terms, subsection (1) of the statute vests the authority to regulate all of the listed activities and things related to firearms exclusively in the Legislative Assembly. Subsection (2) of the statute goes on to specifically prohibit counties, cities and other municipal corporations and districts from enacting civil or criminal ordinances regulating the same activities and things related to firearms. The only exception to the preemption of subsection (1) and the prohibition in subsection (2) is through express authorization by state statute. For authority to be express it must be explicitly stated that the entity can exercise some sort of

---

[1] In 2001, the Legislative Assembly amended ORS 174.020 to expressly allow parties to offer legislative history to "assist a court in its construction of a statute." ORS 174.020 (1)(b). The amendments further provided that the court could limit consideration of legislative history to information provided by the parties and directed courts to "give the weight to the legislative history that the court considers to be appropriate." ORS 174.020 (3). It is not clear if the effect of the 2001 amendments is to allow courts to consider legislative history at the first level of analysis under Portland General Electric. See Smith v. Salem-Keizer School District and Fair Dismissal Appeals Board, 186 Or. App. 237, 245 (2003) and Stevens v. Czerniak, 336 Or. 392, n.12 (2004).

ORS 174.020 provides:
174.020 (1)(a) In the construction of a statute, a court shall pursue the intention of the legislature if possible.
(b) To assist a court in its construction of a statute, a party may offer the legislative history of the statute.
(2) When a general and particular provision are inconsistent, the latter is paramount to the former so that a particular intent controls a general intent that is inconsistent with the particular intent.
(3) A court may limit its consideration of legislative history to the information that the parties provide to the court. A court shall give the weight to the legislative history that the court considers to be appropriate.

regulatory authority over firearms. Therefore, unless there is a statute that explicitly says that some entity may regulate firearms in some manner, it may not do so.

ORS 166.171 to 166.176 are examples of such express grants of authority. ORS 166.173 authorizes cities and counties to adopt ordinances to regulate the possession of loaded firearms in public places. The statute also provides that such an ordinance does not apply to or affect certain listed persons, including a person licensed to carry a concealed handgun.

A. School districts and community college districts

For purposes of your inquiry, one should note that ORS 166.170 (2) specifically includes districts. Because "district" is not defined for purposes of ORS 166.170, the term must be given its ordinary meaning and includes school districts and community college districts. It is also important to note that the express authority granted by ORS 166.173 to regulate possession of loaded firearms in public places is given only to cities and counties and not to districts.

Although district school boards are given general rulemaking authority for the governance of their schools, ORS 332.107, and for the use of their school buildings for civic and recreational purposes, ORS 332.172, and the boards of education of a community college districts are given authority over the grounds and buildings of their districts, ORS 341.290, none of these statutes constitutes express authority to regulate firearms. The statutes do not mention firearms. At best, one could argue that such authority could be implied from the statutes; however, implied authority is not express authority and therefore is not sufficient under ORS 166.170.

Because they lack the express statutory authority required by ORS 166.170, district school boards and boards of education of community college districts may not prohibit a person from carrying a permitted weapon in their schools or on their school grounds.

B. State university system

We do not believe the answer changes when the entity enacting the regulation is a part of state, rather than local, government. Although the specific prohibition contained in ORS 166.170 (2) is directed to units of local government and one might argue that by not listing state agencies the legislature did not intend to prohibit them from enacting regulations relating to firearms, the better reading of the text and context of the statute is that the prohibition in ORS 166.170 (2) does not limit the general preemption language of ORS 166.170 (1), that ORS 166.170 (1) is intended to occupy the field and that, in the absence of express statutory authority, the statute does not leave room in which state agencies may regulate firearms. ORS 166.170 (1) does not vest authority to regulate firearms in "the state" or in "state government"; it vests that authority in the Legislative Assembly.

The context of ORS 166.170 lends weight to this reading. The Legislative Assembly has recognized the importance of and dealt specifically with the issue of possession of firearms on school, college and university property. ORS 166.370 prohibits the possession of firearms while in or on a public building. "Public building" includes public schools, colleges and universities. ORS 166.360. Violation of ORS 166.370 is a Class C felony. The Legislative Assembly also made the policy decision to allow certain persons, including those with concealed handgun licenses, to possess their firearms while in or on a public building without running afoul of ORS 166.370.

Giving ORS 166.170 (1) the meaning dictated by its terms does not leave a regulatory gap regarding possession of firearms at educational institutions. The Legislative Assembly has enacted legislation to cover that situation. Therefore, unless one can find the express statutory authorization required by ORS 166.170 (1), regulation by some entity other than the Legislative Assembly is not allowed.

The Oregon University System is governed by the State Board of Higher Education, which is given general authority to control the grounds and buildings in the system, ORS 351.060, and to adopt rules for the government of institutions under its control, ORS 351.070. Pursuant to this authority, the board has adopted OAR 580-022-0045 (3), which provides that sanctions may be imposed against any person possessing or using firearms on the grounds owned or controlled by an institution of higher education. The prohibition in the rule appears to apply to persons, such as concealed handgun licensees, who could possess a firearm on university grounds without incurring criminal liability under ORS 166.370.

We believe that ORS 166.170 (1) preempts the authority of the State Board of Higher Education to adopt OAR 580-022-0045 (3). The authority given to the board to control the use of its property and to govern its institutions is not the express authority that is needed to overcome ORS 166.170 (1).

2. Other weapons

Although the Legislative Assembly has chosen to prohibit possession of any "instrument used as a dangerous weapon" in schools, ORS 166.370, it has not enacted legislation prohibiting the possession of weapons generally on school property. We have found nothing to indicate that by not enacting such legislation the legislature intended to affirmatively permit such conduct. We find no language relating to weapons other than firearms that is similar to the preemption language in ORS 166.170 (1). Therefore, we do not believe that the legislature has occupied the field regarding the regulation of weapons other than firearms. Under the general statutory authority given to district school boards, boards of education of community college districts and the State Board of Higher Education to adopt rules for the governance of their buildings and grounds, such entities can adopt policies or rules that would prohibit the possession of permitted weapons other than firearms on their property.

Conclusion

Using the process established in Portland General Electric, we interpret ORS 166.170 to mean that district school boards, boards of education of community college districts and the State Board of Higher Education do not have authority to prohibit a person from carrying a firearm on the campuses of the schools, colleges and institutions for which they are responsible. We also conclude that they do have authority to regulate possession of weapons other than firearms on their property.

The opinions written by the Legislative Counsel and the staff of the Legislative Counsel's office are prepared solely for the purpose of assisting members of the Legislative Assembly in the development and consideration of legislative matters. In performing their duties, the Legislative Counsel and the members of the staff of the Legislative Counsel's office have no authority to provide legal advice to any other person, group or entity. For this reason, this opinion should not be considered or used as legal advice by any person other than legislators in the conduct of legislative business. Public bodies and their officers and employees should seek and rely upon the advice and opinion of the Attorney General, district attorney, county counsel, city attorney or other retained counsel. Constituents and other private persons and entities should seek and rely upon the advice and opinion of private counsel.

Very truly yours,

GREGORY A. CHAIMOV
Legislative Counsel

By

Virginia R. Vanderbilt
Senior Deputy Legislative Counsel

STATE OF OREGON
DEPARTMENT OF STATE POLICE
FIREARMS UNIT
3772 PORTLAND RD NE
SALEM OREGON 97303

TOLL-FREE FOR FIREARM TRANSFER BACKGROUND CHECKS 1-800-432-5059 QUESTIONS REGARDING THE PROGRAM PLEASE CALL (503) 378-3070. TOLL-FREE PHONE LINES OPERATIONAL 7 DAYS A WEEK FROM 8A.M. TO 10 P.M. EXCEPT THANKSGIVING AND CHRISTMAS DAY.

ALL ENTRIES MUST BE IN INK

FIREARMS TRANSFER RECORD

SECTION A – TO BE COMPLETED PERSONALLY BY TRANSFEREE (BUYER)

TRANSFEREE (BUYER) INFORMATION

1. NAME _____ 2. DATE OF BIRTH _____

3. RACE _____ 4. SEX _____ 5. SOCIAL SECURITY NUMBER (Optional) _____

6. ADDRESS _____ CITY _____ ST ____ ZIP _____

ELIGIBILITY CERTIFICATION OF TRANSFEREE (BUYER)

NOTE: Questions 7 through 22 must be answered by circling the "yes" or "no" to the right of the question.

ANSWERS

7. Are you the actual buyer of the firearm(s) indicated on this form? .... YES   NO

8. Have you ever been convicted of a felony crime? .... YES   NO

9. Are you currently under indictment or information in any court for a Felony Crime? .... YES   NO

10. Are you a fugitive from justice? (Do you have any out of state warrants?) .... YES   NO

11. Is there an active felony warrant for your arrest? .... YES   NO

12. Are you an unlawful user of, or addicted to, marijuana, or any depressant, stimulant, or narcotic drug, any

    other controlled substance? .... YES   NO

13. Have you ever been adjudicated mentally defective or have you been civilly or criminally committed

    to a mental institution? .... YES   NO

14. Have you been discharged from the Armed Forces under dishonorable conditions? .... YES   NO

15. Are you an alien illegally in the United States? .... YES   NO

16. Have your ever renounced your United States citizenship? .... YES   NO

17. Are you subject to a court order restraining you from harassing, stalking, or threatening an intimate

    partner or child of such partner? .... YES   NO

18. Have you been convicted in any court of a misdemeanor crime of domestic violence? .... YES   NO

19. Have you been convicted or found not guilty by reason of insanity during the previous four years for

    any of the following misdemeanor crimes; Assault 4th Degree, Menacing, Strangulation,

    Intimidation 2nd Degree (1)(b), or Recklessly Endangering? .... YES   NO

20 Are you currently on probation, or by order of a court, prohibited to purchase/possess firearms? .... YES   NO

21 Are you a citizen of the United States? .... YES   NO

22. What is your State of residence? _____ A State of residence is determined for non citizens of the

United States only after you have resided in the State for at least 90 days prior to the date of this sale.

I CERTIFY THE ABOVE ANSWERS ARE TRUE AND CORRECT. I UNDERSTAND A PERSON WHO INDICATES "YES" TO QUESTIONS 8 THROUGH 20 IS PROHIBITED FROM PURCHASING OR POSSESSING A FIREARM. I ALSO UNDERSTAND THAT THE MAKING OF A FALSE ORAL OR WRITTEN STATEMENT OR THE EXHIBITING OF ANY FALSE OR MISREPRESENTED IDENTIFICATION WITH RESPECT TO THIS TRANSACTION IS A CRIME PUNISHABLE AS A CLASS A MISDEMEANOR.

TRANSFEREE'S (Buyer's) SIGNATURE _____ DATE_____

OSP-WBIN2000 (08/00)

TRANSFEROR (SELLER) INFORMATION   LOCATION OF TRANSFER

23. NAME _____   26. BUILDING _____
24. ADDRESS _____   27. ADDRESS _____
    CITY _____ St _____ ZIP _____   CITY _____ St ___ ZIP _____
25. PHONE _____   28. PHONE _____

NOTE: REFER TO INSTRUCTIONS FOR GATHERING THE NECESSARY IDENTIFICATION REQUIRED OR CONTACT THE OREGON STATE POLICE FIREARMS UNIT.
29. TYPE OF IDENTIFICATION PRESENTED BY TRANSFEREE (Buyer) _____

29a. IDENTIFICATION NUMBER _____ EXPIRATION DATE_____

29.b TYPES AND DATES OF ADDITIONAL IDENTIFICATION _____

30. TYPE OF FIREARM(S) TO BE TRANSFERRED:
    ☐ HANDGUN   ☐ LONG GUN   ☐ BOTH

31. MANUFACTURE/ IMPORTER	32. MODEL	33. SERIAL NO.	34. TYPE (Pistol, Revolver, Rifle, Shotgun, etc.)	35.CALIBER/ GAUGE

36. INITIAL RESPONSE BY THE OREGON STATE POLICE FIREARMS UNIT WAS:
    ☐ APPROVED   TRANSACTION APPROVAL NUMBER _____
    ☐ DENIED
    ☐ PENDED/DELAYED   TRANSACTION PENDING DATE _____ EXTENDED UNTIL _____
                                                    (Due)
37. IF INITIAL RESPONSE WAS "PENDED/DELAYED," THE FOLLOWING RESPONSE WAS RECEIVED FROM THE
OREGON STATE POLICE ON _____
                        (Date)
    ☐ APPROVED   TRANSACTION APPROVAL NUMBER_____ (See Section C)
    ☐ DENIED

*** A TRANSACTION APPROVAL NUMBER IS REQUIRED BEFORE FIREARM(S) CAN BE TRANSFERRED ***
THE UNIQUE APPROVAL NUMBER IS ONLY VALID FOR 24 HOURS FROM TIME OF ISSUANCE

Based on transferee's statements in Section A, the verification of identity indicated in items 29. through 29b. the information provided with this form addressing the current State and Federal Laws, it is my understanding that it is not unlawful for me to transfer ownership of the firearm(s) listed in items 31 through 35 to the individual identified in Section A.

38. TRANSFEROR'S (Seller's) SIGNATURE _____ DATE _____

If transaction was Pended/Delayed and the transfer of firearm(s) takes place on a different date other than that which the transferee completed and signed SECTION A, then the transferee needs to sign and date SECTION C, re-certifying SECTION A is still true and correct.

40. TRANSFEREE'S (Buyer's) SIGNATURE _____ DATE _____

136   *Understanding Oregon Gun Laws*

STATE OF OREGON
DEPARTMENT OF STATE POLICE
FIREARMS UNIT
3772 PORTLAND RD NE
SALEM OREGON 97303

PRIVACY ACT INFORMATION
1. AUTHORITY – Solicitation of this information is authorized under ORS 166.436 and ORS 166.438
2. PURPOSE – To determine eligibility of the transferee *(Buyer)* to receive firearms under State and Federal Law.
3. Disclosure of the individual's Social Security Number is strictly voluntary.

FIREARMS TRANSFER RECORD INSTRUCTION SHEET

IMPORTANT REQUIREMENTS

1. A background check for a firearms transfer is required at "Gun Shows," defined as an event where more than 25 firearms are on site and available for transfer.
2. Transferor (seller) must receive notification transferee (buyer) is qualified before transfer is completed.
3. Transferor (seller) may opt to complete the transfer through a Federally Licensed Gun Dealer.
4. The Transferor (seller) shall retain the completed form for at least five years and shall make the completed form available to law enforcement agencies for the purpose of criminal investigations.
5. Pursuant to ORS166.438, Failure to comply with the Criminal History Record Check as defined in ORS166.436 is a Class A misdemeanor, and is punishable on the third and subsequent convictions as a Class C felony.

INSTRUCTIONS TO TRANSFEREE (BUYER)

1. The transferee *(buyer)* of a firearm must personally complete Section A of this form and certify *(sign)* that the answers are true and correct (See Definitions for Eligibility). However, if the buyer is unable to read and/or write, other persons may write the answers, excluding the dealer. Two persons *(other than the dealer)* must then sign as witnesses to the buyer's answers and signature.
2. When the transferee (buyer) of a firearm(s) is a corporation, company, association, partnership or other such business entity, an officer authorized to act on behalf of the business must complete and sign Section A and a written statement, executed under penalties of perjury, stating (A) that the firearm(s) being acquired are for the use of and will be the property of that business entity, and (B) the name and address of that entity.
3. If the transfer of the firearm(s) takes place on a different day from the date that the purchaser signed Section A, then the transferor (seller) must again check the photo ID of the purchaser prior to the transfer, and the purchaser must complete the certification in Section C at the time of transfer.

INSTRUCTIONS TO TRANSFEROR (SELLER)

1. KNOW YOUR CUSTOMER – Before you may sell or deliver a firearm to another person, you must establish the identity, place of residence, and age of the buyer. The buyer must provide a valid government issued photo identification to the seller that contains the buyer's name, residence address and date of birth. A driver's license or ID card issued by the State would be an example. If the identification presented does not include the current address of the transferee (buyer), the transferee (buyer) shall present a second piece of current government-issued identification that contains the current address of the transferee. An acceptable second piece of identification would be a voter's registration card or vehicle registration that supports residence.
2. Prior to transferring a firearm to a purchaser, you must contact the Oregon State Police Firearms Unit for a criminal background check on the transferee (buyer). After the purchaser has completed Section A of the form, and you have completed Section B, you should contact the Firearms Unit at 1-800-432-5059 to initiate a background check. Record the date of contact on line 36 as well as the initial response from the background check of "Approved," "Denied," or "Pended" in the blocks provided. If "Approved," a transaction number will be given to record on the form. This transaction number is your approval from the State to proceed with the sale. **A transaction approval number is required before any firearm(s) can be transferred.** If you receive a Pended response, the transaction will be delayed for further research. Record the "Pend" in the appropriate block and annotate the date of pend as well as the date the Firearms Unit will call you back with a response to the background query. If you receive a "Denial," check the appropriate block. An approval number is a permit valid for 24 hours, if transfer is not completed within that period; a new background check must be initiated.
3. Section C is to be completed if the transfer takes place on a later date than that which the transferee completed and signed Section A. After the transferee certifies that the information in Section A is still accurate.

SECTION A – DEFINITIONS FOR ELIGIBILITY

Reference numbers

7.   Federal firearm laws require the person completing this form to be purchasing the firearm for themselves or as a gift.

8.   Regardless of when or for what, a person who has been convicted of a felony crime is prohibited to purchase a firearm. Prohibition does not apply if such conviction has been expunged or set aside, or the individual's civil rights have been restored.

9.   An indictment or information is a formal accusation of a crime made by a prosecuting attorney.

14.   A dishonorable discharge from the Armed Forces prohibits the purchase of a firearm.

17.   Firearms may not be sold to individuals who have a court order restraining them from harassing, stalking or threatening an intimate partner or child of such intimate partner or person; which was issued after a hearing in which such individual has received actual notice and had an opportunity to participate.

18.   A misdemeanor crime of domestic violence includes, an element of the use or attempted use of physical force, or the threatened use of a deadly weapon, by a current or former spouse, parent or guardian of the victim, by a person with whom the victim shares a child in common, by a person who is cohabiting with or has cohabited with the victim as a spouse, parent or guardian, or by a person similarly situated to a spouse, parent, or guardian of the victim.

20.   Under conditions of probation, ORS 137.540 condition "L", an individual on probation is prohibited to possess firearms, unless the court has specifically deleted the condition.

22.   A non-dealer may only sell a firearm to a resident of his State if the buyer is not prohibited by law from receiving or possessing a firearm, or to a licensee in any State per Federal law.

FEES

1.   The fee for a background check shall not exceed $10.00 and will be charged regardless of transaction being approved, denied or pended.

2.   A reduced fee will be applied to subsequent criminal background checks on the same recipient that are performed during the same day between the hours of 8 a.m. and 10 p.m.

3.   Background check fees are per individual and not based per firearm.

IN THE CIRCUIT COURT OF THE COUNTY OF

_____

Petitioner,

v.

_____, Sheriff of

_____ County, in his
official capacity,

Respondent.

)
)
)
)
)
)
)
)
)
)

No. _____

PETITION TO RESCIND FIREARMS RESTRICTION (ORS 166.274)
ORAL ARGUMENT REQUESTED

Petitioner _____, moves the Court for an Order rescinding the firearms restriction imposed in the above-captioned case. Pursuant to UTCR 4.050, petitioner estimates argument on this matter will take approximately one hour. In support of this motion, petitioner relies upon the points and authorities listed below, the attached affidavit, and other information and authority to be elicited at the hearing on this motion.

POINTS AND AUTHORITIES
ORS 166.274
ORS 166.250

Respectfully submitted this ____ day of _____, 20XX

_____

(Signature of petitioner)

FOR [COUNTY NAME] COUNTY

In the matter of the Concealed Handgun	)	Court Number
License of [Name]	)	PETITION FOR REVIEW OF THE
	)	REVOCATION OF CONCEALED
	)	HANDGUN LICENSE

COMES NOW [Your Name], *pro se*, to petition for judicial review of [County

name] County Sheriff [Sheriff's name]'s [Date of revocation letter] revocation of the

concealed handgun license of [Your Name]. A copy of the [Date of revocation letter]

revocation letter is attached. Please note that the [Date of revocation letter] letter was

served upon [Your Name] on [Date of delivery].

This petition is filed pursuant to ORS 166.293 (3)(b), (5), (6), (8), and (9).

Dated:

_____

[Name], petitioner *pro se*

[Address]

[City, State, Zip]

[Phone number]

CERTIFICATE OF SERVICE

I certify that on _____, 20xx, I served a true and correct copy of my Petition for Revocation of Firearms Restriction and supporting affidavit on _____ by delivering it to the office of _____ and leaving it with the person apparently in charge of the office.

Signature of person making service_____

APPLICATION TO JOIN
Oregon Firearms Federation

Count Me In

Name: _____

Address: _____

City: _____

State: _____Zip: _____

Phone: _____

Email: _____

Enclosed is my contribution.

❑ $20   ❑ $50   ❑ Other:

❑ $30   ❑ $100 $_____

❑ Check ❑ Mastercard ❑ American Express
        ❑ VISA   ❑ Discover

Acct# _____

Exp. date: _____

Signature of cardholder_____

Thank You for Your Support

OFF (Oregon Firearms Federation)
P.O. Box 556, Canby, OR 97013

Phone: 503-263-5830
Email: info@oregonfirearms.org
www.oregonfirearms.org

"Starrett draws on his years of experience representing gun owners through the Oregon Firearms Federation and Gun Owners of America. He understands and has captured the critically important elements of Oregon gun law in clear, easy-to-understand language. If you want to know what your gun rights and responsibilities are, his book is indispensable."

—Alan Korwin, Author
Gun Laws of America

"Kevin's book, Understanding Oregon's Gun Laws, is long overdue and is simply the finest compendium regarding the ownership, possession, and legal use of firearms in the State of Oregon.

Kevin needs no introduction. He is, beyond a doubt, one of the most qualified individuals to write this book. He has tenaciously and selflessly labored to fight and protect Oregonians' rights to possess and use firearms and has earned the right to publish such a momentous work.

This book should be in the hands of every gun owner in Oregon and, in particular, those who visit and commute with firearms within the borders of Oregon. Although no particular book, training video or DVD can ever fully replace competent legal counsel with an attorney—or substitute for continuous hands-on training with a qualified instructor or school—Kevin's work should be used to augment such counsel and/or training and used when such options are not available.

Our recommendation to students at Oregon Firearms Academy is: Always keep this resource nearby, refer to it often, buy and give a copy of it to every freedom loving Oregonian you know!"

Highly recommended!

—Dan Abbott and 1st Sgt. Rick Benson (Ret)
Oregon Firearms Academy